best-ever HOLIDAY

KRAFT®

Recipe Collection

Holiday time means it's time to start thinking of celebrations with the ones you love. Whether your gatherings are big or small, fancy or casual, Kraft helps you plan and prepare for the festive days ahead with *Kraft Best-Ever Holiday Recipe Collection*. Recognizing the many different celebrations of the season, this book offers ideas for Thanksgiving, Hanukkah, Kwanzaa, Christmas and New Year's, plus a bonus section on Halloween. For busy weeknight meals, help is here in a section of extra-easy main dishes. You'll also find a wide selection of simple snacks, gifts from the kitchen, holiday baked goods, enticing side dishes and delightful desserts. You're sure to turn to this irresistible collection of food ideas and hints over and over during the holiday season.

CONTENTS

© Kraft Foods, Inc. and Meredith Corporation, 1999.
All rights reserved.
Produced by Meredith® Books,
1716 Locust St., Des Moines, IA 50309-3023.
Printed in the United States of America.
Library of Congress Catalog Card Number: 99-70533
ISBN: 0-696-21046-0

TACO BELL and HOME ORIGINALS are registered trademarks owned and
licensed by Taco Bell Corp.

Shown on front cover: Heavenly Mint Chocolate Cake (tip, page 72),
Raisin Thumbprint Cookies (recipe, page 149), Miniature Cheesecakes (recipe,
page 63) and Sparkling Raspberry Cranberry Punch (recipe, page 39)

Festive Roasted Pepper
Dip (recipe, page 7)

Chili Cheese Dip
(recipe, page 6)

Ideas for Prepared
Dips (tip, page 7)

Bacon-Cheddar Appetizers
(recipe, page 18)

SNACKS IN MINUTES

"**C**ome over to our house" is all

friends need to hear to drop in after

shopping or choosing a tree. Or, maybe the

invitation's even more impromptu, as

friends deliver gifts and greetings. Either

way, with Kraft products and these

delightfully easy ideas for enjoying them,

you'll never be caught empty-handed.

Chili Cheese Dip

(Photo on pages 4–5.)

Prep time: 5 minutes   Baking time: 25 minutes

Makes 8 to 10 servings

1   **package (8 ounces) PHILADELPHIA Cream Cheese, softened**
1   **can (15 ounces) chili without beans**
1   **cup KRAFT Shredded Sharp Cheddar Cheese**

Spread cream cheese on bottom of 9-inch pie plate or quiche dish. Top with chili and cheddar cheese.

Bake at 350°F for 20 to 25 minutes or until thoroughly heated. Garnish with chopped green onion and tomato. Serve with tortilla chips.

Holiday Take-Along Tidbits

When you are bringing a cold appetizer to a party, chill it at home in advance and keep it cold with an ice pack during your traveling time. Hot foods are best if they are prepared, but not heated. Check with the hostess to make sure it's okay to do the last-minute baking or heating once you arrive. Remember to bring any needed serving utensils.

Festive Roasted *Pepper* Dip

(Photo on pages 4–5.)

Prep time: 10 minutes plus refrigerating

Makes 3 cups

1 **cup BREAKSTONE'S *or* KNUDSEN Sour Cream**	**Mix** all ingredients. Refrigerate.
1 **cup KRAFT Mayo Light Mayonnaise**	**Serve** with assorted cut-up vegetables.
1 **jar (7½ ounces) roasted red peppers, drained, finely chopped**	
1 **can (4 ounces) chopped green chilies, drained**	
1 **tablespoon lemon juice**	
½ **teaspoon garlic powder**	

Ideas for Prepared Dips

Keep prepared KRAFT sour cream dips on hand so you'll always be ready to entertain on a moment's notice. You can find these dips in a variety of flavors in the dairy case at your local supermarket. To go beyond the classic duo of chips and dip, try these exciting ideas:

• Serve garlic bagel chips, breadsticks, toasted pita bread triangles, pretzel rods and big chewy pretzels for a new twist in dippers.

• Enhance the holiday crudité platter with sweet potato rounds, rutabaga and fennel slices, jicama cubes, asparagus spears and Belgian endive leaves.

• Spoon KRAFT French Onion Dip into hollowed-out cherry tomatoes or steamed small red potatoes.

• Serve your favorite KRAFT dips in containers such as hollowed-out round bread loaves, pepper shells or acorn squash halves.

Italian Vegetable Dip
(recipe opposite page)

Savory Spinach Dip
(recipe opposite page)

Savory Spinach Dip

Prep time: 5 minutes   Stovetop cooking time: 10 minutes or Microwave time: 8 minutes

Makes 2 cups

2 slices OSCAR MAYER Bacon, finely chopped
⅓ cup chopped red pepper
1 clove garlic, minced
1 package (10 ounces) frozen chopped spinach, cooked, well drained
1 jar (8 ounces) CHEEZ WHIZ Pasteurized Process Cheese Sauce
½ cup BREAKSTONE'S *or* KNUDSEN Sour Cream

Cook and stir bacon in saucepan on medium heat until crisp; drain. Add red pepper and garlic. Cook 1 minute or until tender.

Stir in remaining ingredients. Cook, stirring constantly, until thoroughly heated.

Serve with Italian bread cubes or assorted crackers.

To microwave: Microwave bacon in 1-quart microwavable bowl on HIGH 1 to 2 minutes or until crisp; drain.

Stir in red pepper and garlic. Microwave 1 minute or until tender.

Stir in remaining ingredients. Microwave on MEDIUM (50%) 4 to 5 minutes or until thoroughly heated, stirring every minute.

Italian *Vegetable* Dip

Prep time: 10 minutes plus refrigerating

Makes 2¼ cups

1 cup BREAKSTONE'S *or* KNUDSEN Sour Cream
1 cup KRAFT Mayo Real Mayonnaise
1 envelope GOOD SEASONS Zesty Italian Salad Dressing Mix
¼ cup finely chopped green pepper
¼ cup finely chopped red pepper

Mix sour cream, mayo and salad dressing mix. Stir in green and red pepper. Refrigerate.

Serve with assorted cut-up vegetables, boiled potatoes, breadsticks or chips.

Cheesy Beer Dip

Prep time: 5 minutes Microwave time: 2 minutes

Makes 2 cups

1 jar (16 ounces) CHEEZ WHIZ Pasteurized
    Process Cheese Sauce
⅓ **cup beer**

Microwave process cheese sauce as directed on label.

Mix process cheese sauce and beer in bowl, stirring until mixture becomes smooth. Garnish with sliced fresh chives. Serve with pretzels and/or breadsticks.

Cheese and Nut *Roll*

Prep time: 20 minutes plus refrigerating

Makes 10 to 12 servings

1   package (8 ounces) PHILADELPHIA Cream
    Cheese, softened
1½ cups KRAFT Shredded Cheddar Cheese
2   tablespoons milk
2   tablespoons *each* finely chopped green
    onion and finely chopped red pepper
1   envelope GOOD SEASONS Garlic & Herb
    or Italian Salad Dressing Mix
½   cup finely chopped pecans

Mix cream cheese, cheddar cheese and milk with electric mixer on medium speed until well blended. Add onion, red pepper and salad dressing mix; mix well. Refrigerate 30 minutes.

Shape cheese mixture into 8-inch roll.* Cover with pecans. Refrigerate several hours. Serve with crackers.

*Note: To shape, place cheese mixture on sheet of plastic wrap; form into roll. Sprinkle with pecans, securing to top and sides of roll by pressing in with plastic wrap.

Festive Appetizer Spread

Prep time: 15 minutes plus refrigerating

Makes 2 cups

2 **packages (8 ounces *each*) PHILADELPHIA
Cream Cheese, softened**
1 **jar (8 ounces) CHEEZ WHIZ Pasteurized
Process Cheese Sauce**
¼ **cup *each* chopped red pepper and
sliced green onions**
2 **teaspoons Worcestershire sauce**

Mix all ingredients with electric mixer on medium speed until well blended. Refrigerate.

Garnish with chopped nuts, parsley or fresh vegetable cutouts. Serve with assorted crackers, breads, breadsticks or cut-up vegetables.

Edible Serving Containers

Look no further than your vegetable or fruit drawer for fun and easy ways to serve holiday food. Use pepper shells to hold celery and carrot sticks. Hollow out red or green cabbage to make a bowl for dip. Scallop orange shells or melon halves to make individual bowls for fruit salad.

PHILADELPHIA® 7-Layer *Mexican* Dip

Prep time: 10 minutes plus refrigerating

Makes 6 to 8 servings

1	**package (8 ounces) PHILADELPHIA Cream Cheese, softened**
1	**tablespoon taco seasoning mix**
1	**cup prepared guacamole**
1	**cup TACO BELL HOME ORIGINALS Thick 'N Chunky Salsa**
1	**cup shredded lettuce**
1	**cup KRAFT Shredded Sharp Cheddar Cheese**
½	**cup chopped green onions**
2	**tablespoons sliced pitted ripe olives**

Mix cream cheese and seasoning mix. Spread on bottom of 9-inch pie plate or quiche dish.

Layer remaining ingredients over cream cheese mixture. Refrigerate.

Garnish with cherry tomatoes and fresh herb. Serve with tortilla chips.

Veggie Pizza Appetizers

Prep time: 15 minutes plus refrigerating   Baking time: 13 minutes

Makes 24

2   cans (8 ounces *each*) refrigerated crescent dinner rolls

1   package (8 ounces) PHILADELPHIA Cream Cheese, softened

½   cup BREAKSTONE'S *or* KNUDSEN Sour Cream

1   envelope GOOD SEASONS Gourmet Parmesan Italian *or* Italian Salad Dressing Mix

5   cups cut-up assorted fresh vegetables

1   cup KRAFT Shredded Cheddar Cheese

Unroll dough into 4 rectangles. Press onto bottom and sides of 15×10×1-inch baking pan to form crust.

Bake at 375°F for 11 to 13 minutes or until golden brown; cool.

Mix cream cheese, sour cream and salad dressing mix until well blended. Spread on crust. Top with remaining ingredients. Refrigerate. Cut into squares.

Speed-Soften Cream Cheese

Did you forget to take the PHILADELPHIA Cream Cheese out of the refrigerator to soften? No problem. Simply pop the unwrapped cream cheese into the microwave oven on HIGH for a few seconds until it becomes soft enough to combine easily with other ingredients. Allow 5 to 10 seconds for a 3-ounce package and 15 seconds for an 8-ounce package.

Cinnamon 'n' Apple *Wafers*

Prep time: 15 minutes   Baking time: 5 minutes

Makes 28

½   **cup sugar**
½   **teaspoon ground cinnamon**
¼   **teaspoon ground nutmeg**
1   **each small red and green apple, thinly sliced**
28 **shredded whole wheat wafer crackers**
1   **package (10 ounces) CRACKER BARREL Vermont Sharp-White Natural Cheddar Cheese, thinly sliced**

Mix sugar, cinnamon and nutmeg; toss with apple slices. Place wafers on cookie sheet; top each with 1 cheese slice and 2 apple slices.

Bake at 350°F for 4 to 5 minutes or until cheese is melted. Serve warm.

Cheddar and Onion Bites

Prep time: 10 minutes   Broiling time: 3 minutes

Makes 16

⅓   **cup KRAFT Mayo Real Mayonnaise**
2   **tablespoons chopped green onion**
16 **slices cocktail rye bread, toasted**
1   **package (10 ounces) CRACKER BARREL Sharp Natural Cheddar Cheese, thinly sliced**

Mix mayo and onion. Spread toasted bread slices with mayo mixture. Top with cheese. Place on cookie sheet.

Broil 2 to 3 minutes or until cheese is melted. Garnish as desired.

Note: If you like, substitute rye crackers for toasted cocktail rye bread.

Cheddar and Onion Bites
(recipe opposite page)

Cinnamon 'n'
Apple Wafers
(recipe opposite
page)

Bacon-Cheddar Appetizers

(Photo on pages 4–5.)

Prep time: 20 minutes   Broiling time: 3 minutes

Makes about 5 dozen

1   **package (8 ounces) KRAFT Shredded
     Sharp Cheddar Cheese**
1   **package (8 ounces) OSCAR MAYER
     Bacon, crisply cooked, crumbled**
¼   **cup KRAFT Mayo Real Mayonnaise**
2   **tablespoons finely chopped onion**
½   **teaspoon dry mustard
     Melba toast rounds**

Mix all ingredients except toast rounds until well blended. Spread each toast round with 1 teaspoon cheese mixture. Place on cookie sheet.

Broil 2 to 3 minutes or until cheese is melted. Garnish as desired.

Get Snippy with Bacon

When your recipe calls for crumbled cooked OSCAR MAYER Bacon, cut it before cooking so you won't burn your fingers crumbling the bacon when it's hot. Use kitchen shears to cut through as many slices as you need—no need to separate the slices first.

Toasted *Cheese* Wedges

Prep time: 10 minutes   Broiling time: 3 minutes

Makes 20

1   **package (10 ounces) CRACKER BARREL NEW YORK AGED RESERVE Natural Extra Sharp Cheddar Cheese**
½   **cup Italian-style bread crumbs**
½   **teaspoon crushed red pepper (optional)**
1   **egg, beaten**

Spray cookie sheet with no stick cooking spray.

Cut cheese into ½-inch slices; cut slices diagonally in half. Mix bread crumbs and pepper. Dip cheese in egg; coat with crumb mixture. Place on prepared cookie sheet.

Broil 2 to 3 minutes or until cheese is melted. Serve warm with pizza or spaghetti sauce, if desired.

Little Tacos

Prep time: 5 minutes   Cooking time: 10 minutes

Makes about 50

1   **package (16 ounces) OSCAR MAYER Little Smokies**
1   **jar (8 ounces) CHEEZ WHIZ Pasteurized Process Cheese Sauce**
½   **cup taco sauce**

Heat smokies as directed on package.

Meanwhile, mix process cheese sauce and taco sauce in small saucepan. Cook on medium-low heat 10 minutes or until process cheese sauce melts, stirring frequently.

To serve, place smokies and sauce in fondue pot or slow cooker. Garnish with chopped fresh cilantro or parsley. Keep warm on low heat.

CATALINA® Chicken Wings

Prep time: 5 minutes plus marinating
Baking time: 45 minutes or Grilling time: 20 minutes

Makes about 6 dozen

1   **bottle (16 ounces) KRAFT CATALINA Dressing**
½   **cup soy sauce**
5   **pounds chicken wings, separated at joints, tips discarded, *and/or* chicken drummettes**

Mix dressing and soy sauce; reserve ½ cup of the dressing mixture.

Pour remaining dressing mixture over chicken; cover. Refrigerate several hours or overnight to marinate. Drain; discard marinade.

Place chicken in 15×10×1-inch foil-lined baking pan. Bake at 375°F for 45 minutes or until golden brown, brushing halfway through baking with reserved ½ cup dressing mixture. Serve with blue cheese dressing sprinkled with cracked pepper.

To grill: Prepare as directed, placing chicken on grill over medium coals. Grill 20 minutes or until cooked through, turning once and brushing occasionally with reserved ½ cup dressing mixture.

Little Tacos (recipe opposite page)

CATALINA® Chicken Wings (recipe oppostie page)

Refreshing *Cucumber*, Dill 'n' Cheddar Snacks

Assorted crackers
Cucumber slices
CRACKER BARREL Sharp Natural Cheddar
  Cheese, thinly sliced and cut into
  shapes with cookie cutters
Fresh dill sprigs

Top each cracker with cucumber slice, cheese and dill sprig.

Cranberry Cheddar Turkey Snacks

Prep time: 10 minutes

Makes 20

20 sesame seed *or* table wafer crackers
1 package (10 ounces) CRACKER BARREL Extra Sharp Natural Cheddar Cheese, thinly sliced
½ pound thinly sliced cooked turkey breast
⅓ cup cranberry orange sauce

Top crackers with cheese, turkey and cranberry orange sauce. Garnish with green onion slivers.

Cranberry Cheddar Snacks: Prepare snacks as directed, omitting turkey.

Quick Crabmeat Appetizer

Prep time: 5 minutes

Makes 6 to 8 servings

1   package (8 ounces) PHILADELPHIA Cream
    Cheese, softened
¼   cup SAUCEWORKS Cocktail Sauce
1   package (8 ounces) imitation crabmeat
    or 1 package (6 ounces) frozen
    cooked tiny shrimp, thawed, drained

Spread cream cheese on serving plate.

Pour cocktail sauce over cream cheese; top with imitation crabmeat. Garnish as desired.

Serve with crackers or cocktail rye bread slices.

SUGAR BEAR™ *Snack Mix*

Prep time: 10 minutes   Baking time: 10 minutes plus cooling

Makes 3 cups

4 **cups POST GOLDEN CRISP Sweetened Puffed Wheat Cereal**

½ **cup peanuts**

½ **cup raisins**

2 **tablespoons butter *or* margarine, melted**

½ **teaspoon ground cinnamon**

Mix cereal, peanuts and raisins in large bowl. Mix butter and cinnamon in small bowl. Pour over cereal mixture; toss well.

Spread evenly in 15×10×1-inch baking pan.

Bake at 350°F for 10 minutes. Cool. Store in tightly covered container.

Easy Snack Mix

Prep time: 5 minutes

Makes about 8 cups

6 **cups POST HONEYCOMB Cereal** *or* **POST ALPHA-BITS Frosted Letter Shaped Oat and Corn Cereal**
1½ **cups miniature marshmallows**
1 **cup raisins**
¼ **cup** *each* **salted peanuts and candy coated chocolate-covered candies**

Mix all ingredients in large bowl.

SPOON SIZE® *Party Mix*

Prep time: 10 minutes   Baking time: 30 minutes or Microwave time: 6 minutes

Makes 6 cups

4 **cups POST SPOON SIZE Shredded Wheat Cereal**
1 **cup popped popcorn**
1 **cup small unsalted pretzels**
3 **tablespoons margarine, melted**
1 **tablespoon Worcestershire sauce**
1 **teaspoon seasoned salt**

Place cereal, popcorn and pretzels in 15×10×1-inch baking pan. Mix margarine, Worcestershire sauce and seasoned salt. Drizzle evenly over cereal mixture; toss to coat.

Bake at 300°F for 30 minutes or until crisp, stirring halfway through baking time. Cool. Store in tightly covered container.

To microwave: Prepare as directed, tossing mixture in large microwavable bowl. Microwave on HIGH for 5 to 6 minutes or until crisp, stirring halfway through cooking time. Cool.

Easy Snack Mix
(recipe opposite page)

SPOON SIZE® Party Mix
(recipe opposite page)

Roast turkey
(tip, page 33)

Souper Rice
(recipe, page 39)

Glazed sweet potatoes

Cranberry Holiday Mold
(recipe, page 40)

MEMORABLE MENUS FOR THE SEASON

Thanksgiving starts off a whole season of festive feasting. These complete holiday menus keep the preparations simple and the food memorable.

- Easy-Does-It Thanksgiving Feast

- Mix-and-Match Christmas Dinner

- Holiday Open House

- Holiday Brunch

- Hanukkah Gathering

- Kwanzaa Dinner

- New Year's Gala

- Big Bowl Bash

Easy Potato
Bake (recipe,
page 34)

Classic Green
Bean Casserole
(recipe, page 36)

Easy-Does-It Thanksgiving Feast

Cheese and Pesto Toasts
Hot Artichoke Dip
Roast turkey
Easy Potato Bake
Classic Green Bean Casserole
Kir Royale Mold
Fluffy 2-Step Cheesecake

Cheese and Pesto *Toasts*

Prep time: 10 minutes   Broiling time: 3 minutes

Makes 15

15 slices Italian bread, lightly toasted
½ cup prepared pesto sauce
30 slices plum tomato (about 5 medium tomatoes)
1 package (10 ounces) CRACKER BARREL Extra Sharp Natural Cheddar Cheese, thinly sliced

Spread toasted bread slices with pesto sauce. Top each toast slice with 2 tomato slices and 1 cheese slice. Place on cookie sheet.

Broil 2 to 3 minutes or until cheese is melted.

Hot *Artichoke* Dip

Prep time: 10 minutes   Baking time: 25 minutes

Makes 2 cups

1   **can (14 ounces) artichoke hearts,
    drained, chopped**
1   **cup (4 ounces) KRAFT 100% Grated
    Parmesan Cheese**
1   **cup KRAFT Mayo Real Mayonnaise *or*
    MIRACLE WHIP Salad Dressing**
1   **clove garlic, minced
    Chopped tomato
    Sliced fresh chives**

Mix all ingredients except tomato
and chives.

Spoon into 9-inch pie plate or quiche
dish.

Bake at 350°F for 20 to 25 minutes or
until lightly browned. Sprinkle with tomato
and chives. Serve with crackers.

Spicy Artichoke Dip: Prepare as
directed, adding 1 can (4 ounces) chopped
green chilies, drained.

Spinach Artichoke Dip: Prepare
as directed, adding 1 package (10 ounces)
frozen chopped spinach, thawed,
well drained.

To make ahead, prepare as directed
except do not bake; cover. Refrigerate
overnight. Before serving, bake, uncovered,
at 350°F for 20 to 25 minutes or until
lightly browned.

Turkey Roasting Tips

ready-to-cook weight	oven temperature	roasting time
8 to 12 pounds	325°F	2½ to 3¼ hours
12 to 14 pounds	325°F	3 to 3¾ hours
14 to 18 pounds	325°F	3½ to 4 hours
18 to 20 pounds	325°F	3¾ to 4½ hours
20 to 24 pounds	325°F	4¼ to 5 hours

TO PREPARE A TURKEY FOR ROASTING, rinse the bird thoroughly on the outside, as well as inside the body cavity and neck cavity (small hole at top of bird between wings). Pat dry. Rub the inside of the body cavity with salt, if desired. Place quartered onions and celery in body cavity. Pull neck skin to back and fasten with a short skewer. Tuck the drumsticks under the band of skin that crosses the tail. (If there isn't a band, tie drumsticks to tail.) Twist wing tips under back.

PLACE TURKEY, breast side up, on a rack in a shallow roasting pan. Brush with cooking oil and sprinkle with a crushed dried herb, such as thyme or oregano, if desired. Place a meat thermometer in the center of an inside thigh muscle, not touching bone. Cover loosely with foil. Press foil over drumsticks and neck. Roast at 325°F, using timings above.

DURING ROASTING, baste with drippings occasionally, if desired. When bird is ⅔ done, cut skin or string between drumsticks. Remove foil the last 30 to 45 minutes. When done, the thigh meat should be 180°F (the temperature will rise on standing). The meat should be tender and the juices from the thigh should run clear. Remove the turkey from oven; cover loosely with foil. Let stand 20 minutes before carving.

Countdown to a Great Holiday Meal

Take a moment to plan a menu with do-ahead tricks; then create a countdown schedule to ease last-minute kitchen time. Prepare desserts and molded salads a day or two ahead, and assemble ingredients for other recipes. Counting backwards from the time you want the meal on the table, chart out when to start the turkey, potatoes and vegetables. Then relax and enjoy the family.

Easy Potato *Bake*

(Photo on page 30.)

Prep time: 10 minutes   Baking time: 35 minutes

Makes 12 to 16 servings

1   **package (32 ounces) frozen Southern-style hash brown potatoes**
1   **container (16 ounces) BREAKSTONE'S *or* KNUDSEN Sour Cream**
1   **package (8 ounces) KRAFT Shredded Cheddar Cheese**
1   **can (10¾ ounces) condensed cream of chicken soup**
1   **cup *each* chopped green onions and corn flake crumbs**
2   **tablespoons butter *or* margarine, melted**

Mix potatoes, sour cream, cheese, soup and onions in large bowl.

Spoon into greased 13×9-inch baking dish. Toss crumbs and butter; sprinkle over potato mixture.

Bake at 375°F for 35 minutes.

Mexican Style Easy Potato Bake:

Prepare as directed, adding 1 can (4 ounces) chopped green chilies, undrained, to potato mixture. Substitute KRAFT Four Cheese Mexican Style Shredded Cheese for cheddar cheese and 1 cup crushed tortilla chips for corn flake crumbs.

Leftover Magic

Sandwiches, move over. Turkey leftovers take on a fresh, new personality when sliced into other favorite dishes, such as salads, stir-fries, pastas or omelets. Or, top larger slices of meat with a sauce made from canned cream soup and a pinch of herb. Serve with prepared stuffing mix, couscous or mashed potatoes, and yesterday's dinner debuts in a brand-new role.

Kir Royale Mold

Prep time: 15 minutes   Refrigerating time: 4¾ hours

Makes 12 servings

 2 **cups boiling water**
 1 **package (6 ounces) *or* 2 packages**
     (3 ounces *each*) JELL-O Sparkling Wild
     Berry *or* Sparkling White Grape
     Flavor Gelatin Dessert
1½ **cups cold club soda, seltzer *or***
     champagne
 2 **tablespoons crème de cassis liqueur**
     (optional)
 2 **cups raspberries**

Stir boiling water into gelatin in large bowl at least 2 minutes until completely dissolved. Refrigerate 15 minutes. Gently stir in cold club soda and liqueur. Refrigerate about 30 minutes or until slightly thickened. (Gelatin is consistency of unbeaten egg whites.) Gently stir for 15 seconds. Stir in raspberries. Pour into 6-cup mold.

Refrigerate 4 hours or until firm. Unmold (tip, page 216). Garnish with additional raspberries and fresh mint. Store leftover gelatin mold in refrigerator.

Classic *Green Bean* Casserole

(Photo on page 30.)

Prep time: 5 minutes   Baking time: 35 minutes

Makes 8 servings

3 **packages (9 ounces *each)* frozen French cut green beans, thawed, drained**
1 **can (10¾ ounces) condensed cream of mushroom soup**
1 **jar (8 ounces) CHEEZ WHIZ Pasteurized Process Cheese Sauce *or* 1 cup CHEEZ WHIZ LIGHT Pasteurized Process Cheese Product**
⅛ **teaspoon pepper**
1 **can (2.8 ounces) French fried onions, divided**

Mix all ingredients except ½ can onions in 1½-quart casserole.

Bake at 350°F for 30 minutes. Top with remaining ½ can onions. Bake an additional 5 minutes.

To make ahead, prepare as directed except do not bake; cover. Refrigerate overnight. Before serving, bake, uncovered, at 350°F for 45 to 50 minutes or until thoroughly heated, topping with remaining ½ can onions during last 5 minutes of baking time.

Decorating for Thanksgiving

Set the mood for Thanksgiving as you would for other holidays. Plan a family outing to gather leaves, collect pinecones and select colorful gourds, pumpkins and ears of corn. Then carve out time together to transform your home into a harvest of Thanksgiving treasures.

Fluffy 2-Step Cheesecake

Prep time: 15 minutes plus refrigerating

Makes 8 servings

1   package (8 ounces) PHILADELPHIA **Cream Cheese, softened**

⅓   **cup sugar**

1   **tub (8 ounces) COOL WHIP Whipped Topping, thawed**

1   **prepared graham cracker crumb crust (6 ounce *or* 9 inch)**

Beat cream cheese and sugar in large bowl with wire whisk or electric mixer until smooth. Gently stir in whipped topping.

Spoon into crust. Refrigerate 3 hours or until set. Garnish with thin apple slices and curled orange peel. Store leftover cheesecake in refrigerator.

Roast turkey
(tip, page 33)

Cranberry Holiday Mold
(recipe, page 40)

Souper Rice (recipe
opposite page)

Glazed sweet potatoes

Mix-and-Match Christmas Dinner

Roast turkey or baked ham
Souper Rice or Almost Risotto
Herb-Roasted Potatoes or Glazed sweet potatoes (use your favorite recipe)
Cranberry Holiday Mold or Honey Dijon Waldorf Salad
No Bake Cappuccino Cheesecake Cups
or
GERMAN'S® Sweet Chocolate Pie in Coconut Crust
Sparkling Raspberry Cranberry Punch

Souper Rice

(Photo on pages 28–29 and opposite page.)

Prep time: 5 minutes   Cooking time: 5 minutes plus standing

Makes 4 servings

1   **can (10¾ ounces) condensed cream of mushroom soup**
1   **soup can (1⅓ cups) water** *or* **milk**
2   **cups MINUTE White Rice, uncooked**

Boil soup and water in medium saucepan.

Stir in rice; cover. Remove from heat. Let stand 5 minutes. Stir. Garnish with fresh sage leaves.

Sparkling Raspberry Cranberry Punch

(Photo on front cover.)

Prep time: 10 minutes plus refrigerating

Makes 32 (½-cup) servings

1   **tub CRYSTAL LIGHT Raspberry Ice Flavor Low Calorie Soft Drink Mix**
1   **tub CRYSTAL LIGHT Cranberry Breeze Flavor Low Calorie Soft Drink Mix**
8   **cups (2 quarts) cold water**
2   **bottles (1 liter** *each)* **chilled raspberry-flavored seltzer** *or* **seltzer**
1   **package (10 ounces) frozen raspberries, thawed**

Place drink mixes in punch bowl. Add water; stir to dissolve. Cover. Refrigerate.

Stir in seltzer and raspberries just before serving. Garnish with fresh cranberries.

Cranberry Holiday Mold

(Photo on pages 28–29 and 38.)

Prep time: 20 minutes plus refrigerating

Makes 10 servings

2 cups boiling water
1 package (8-serving size) *or* 2 packages
(4-serving size *each*) JELL-O Cranberry
Flavor Gelatin Dessert (*or any red
flavor*)
1½ cups cold ginger ale *or* cold water
2 cups halved seedless green *and/or* red
grapes
1 can (11 ounces) mandarin orange
segments, drained

Stir boiling water into gelatin in large
bowl at least 2 minutes until completely
dissolved. Stir in cold ginger ale. Refrigerate
about 1½ hours or until thickened.
(Spoon drawn through leaves a definite
impression.) Stir in fruit. Spoon into
5-cup mold.

Refrigerate 4 hours or until firm.
Unmold (tip, page 216). Garnish as
desired. Store leftover gelatin mold in
refrigerator.

Almost *Risotto*

Prep time: 5 minutes   Cooking time: 10 minutes

Makes 6 servings

1 can (13¾ ounces) chicken broth
1 envelope GOOD SEASONS Gourmet
Parmesan Italian Salad Dressing Mix
1 cup orzo pasta, uncooked
1 jar (4½ ounces) sliced mushrooms,
drained

Bring broth and salad dressing mix to boil
in medium saucepan on medium-high heat.

Add orzo. Reduce heat to low; cover.
Simmer 10 minutes or until orzo is tender.

Stir in mushrooms. Serve with grated
Parmesan cheese, if desired.

Honey Dijon Waldorf Salad

Prep time: 10 minutes plus refrigerating

Makes 4 servings

2 **cups chopped apples**
½ **cup KRAFT Honey Dijon Dressing**
½ **cup sliced celery**
½ **cup raisins**
¼ **cup chopped walnuts**

Toss all ingredients in large bowl. Refrigerate.

Herb-Roasted Potatoes

Prep time: 15 minutes   Baking time: 40 minutes

Makes 8 servings

½ **cup MIRACLE WHIP Salad Dressing**
1 **tablespoon *each* dried oregano leaves, garlic powder and onion powder**
1 **teaspoon seasoned salt**
1 **tablespoon water**
2 **pounds small red potatoes, quartered**

Mix dressing, seasonings and water in large bowl. Add potatoes; toss to coat. Place potatoes on greased cookie sheet.

Bake at 425°F for 20 minutes. Turn potatoes; continue baking 20 minutes or until crisp and browned.

No Bake Cappuccino Cheesecake Cups

Prep time: 15 minutes plus refrigerating

Makes 12

1 package (11.1 ounces) JELL-O No Bake Real Cheesecake
2 tablespoons sugar
⅓ cup butter *or* margarine, melted
2 teaspoons MAXWELL HOUSE Instant Coffee
1½ cups cold milk
¼ teaspoon ground cinnamon (optional)

Mix Crumbs, sugar and butter thoroughly with fork until crumbs are well moistened. Press onto bottoms of 12 paper-lined muffin cups.

Dissolve coffee in milk. Beat milk mixture, Filling Mix and cinnamon with electric mixer on low speed until blended. Beat on medium speed 3 minutes (filling will be thick). Spoon over crumb mixture in muffin cups.

Refrigerate at least 1 hour or until ready to serve. Garnish with chocolate curls. Store leftover cheesecakes in refrigerator.

GERMAN'S® Sweet Chocolate Pie in *Coconut Crust*

Prep time: 20 minutes plus freezing   Baking time: 30 minutes

Makes 8 servings

1   **package (7 ounces) BAKER'S
    ANGEL FLAKE Coconut (2⅔ cups)**
⅓   **cup butter *or* margarine, melted**
1   **package (4 ounces) BAKER'S GERMAN'S
    Sweet Baking Chocolate**
⅓   **cup milk, divided**
4   **ounces PHILADELPHIA Cream Cheese,
    softened**
2   **tablespoons sugar**
1   **tub (8 ounces) COOL WHIP Whipped
    Topping, thawed**

Mix coconut and butter. Press onto bottom and up sides of 9-inch pie plate. Bake at 350°F for 20 to 30 minutes or until golden brown. Cool on wire rack.

Microwave chocolate and 2 tablespoons of the milk in large microwavable bowl on HIGH 1½ to 2 minutes or until chocolate is almost melted, stirring halfway through heating time. Stir until chocolate is completely melted.

Beat in cream cheese, sugar and remaining milk with wire whisk until well blended. Refrigerate about 10 minutes to cool. Gently stir in whipped topping until smooth. Spoon into crust.

Freeze 4 hours or until firm. Garnish with additional whipped topping, toasted coconut and chocolate candies. Let stand at room temperature about 15 minutes or until pie can be cut easily. Store leftover pie in freezer.

Holiday Open House

Holiday Cheese Tree
Turkey with Sesame Peanut Sauce
Smokie Wraps with Dijon Dipping Sauce
Hot Bacon Cheese Spread
One Bowl Chocolate Fudge
Chocolate Berry Dessert Cups

Holiday *Cheese* Tree

Prep time: 15 minutes plus refrigerating

Makes 12 servings

2 **packages (8 ounces *each*) PHILADELPHIA Cream Cheese, softened**
1 **package (8 ounces) KRAFT Shredded Sharp Cheddar Cheese**
1 **tablespoon *each* chopped red pepper and finely chopped onion**
2 **teaspoons Worcestershire sauce**
1 **teaspoon lemon juice**
Dash ground red pepper

Mix cream cheese and cheddar cheese with electric mixer on medium speed until well blended.

Blend in remaining ingredients. Refrigerate several hours or overnight.

Drop 6 ($\frac{1}{3}$-cup) measures of mixture into triangle shape on serving platter. Drop remaining mixture at base of triangle; smooth to form tree. Garnish with twisted thin lengthwise slices of zucchini, fresh flat-leaf parsley and pomegranate seeds. Serve with toasted bread or crackers.

Turkey with Sesame Peanut Sauce

Prep time: 10 minutes

Makes 40

1   **pound LOUIS RICH Breast of Turkey**
¾   **cup orange marmalade**
¼   **cup peanut butter**
3   **tablespoons teriyaki sauce**
2   **teaspoons toasted sesame seeds**

Cut turkey into bite-size cubes; spear cubes with toothpicks. Garnish with pepper cutouts.

Mix remaining ingredients in small bowl. Stir until well blended. Garnish with green onion strips. Serve sauce as dip for turkey.

Smokie Wraps with Dijon Dipping Sauce (recipe opposite page)

Turkey with Sesame Peanut Sauce (recipe above)

Smokie Wraps with *Dijon* Dipping Sauce

Prep time: 10 minutes   Baking time: 8 minutes

Makes about 4 dozen

⅔   **cup Dijon mustard**
⅓   **cup honey**
10   **flour tortillas (6 inch)**
1   **package (16 ounces) OSCAR MAYER Little Smokies *or* Little Wieners**

Mix mustard and honey in small bowl.

Spread each tortilla lightly with mustard sauce. Cut each tortilla into 6 strips. Roll 1 Little Smokie in each tortilla strip; secure with toothpicks and place on nonstick cookie sheet (or sheet sprayed with no stick cooking spray). Reserve extra mustard sauce for dipping.

Bake at 350°F for 5 to 8 minutes or until hot. Serve with reserved mustard sauce.

Fix-It-Easy Snacks

Little Wieners and Little Smokies are bite-size versions of the regular OSCAR MAYER Wieners and Smokie Links. Serve them as appetizers and snacks or in main dishes. Here are just a few suggestions on how you can enjoy these tiny delicious treats.

• Heat them in a prepared sauce, such as bottled barbecue sauce, canned cheese soup or hot mustard. Serve them with decorative toothpicks for an uncomplicated appetizer.

• Heat and serve them in small dinner rolls or tiny buns made for mini hot dogs.

• Wrap each of them in refrigerated biscuit dough and bake.

Hot Bacon Cheese Spread

Prep time: 15 minutes   Baking time: 1 hour

Makes 3½ cups

1   **loaf (16 ounces) round bread**
12   **slices OSCAR MAYER Center Cut Bacon,
      crisply cooked, crumbled**
1   **package (8 ounces) KRAFT Shredded
      Colby & Monterey Jack Cheese**
1   **cup (4 ounces) KRAFT 100% Grated
      Parmesan Cheese**
1   **cup KRAFT Mayo Real Mayonnaise**
1   **small onion, finely chopped**
1   **clove garlic, minced**

Cut lengthwise slice from top of bread loaf, remove center, leaving 1-inch-thick shell. Cut removed bread into bite-size pieces; set aside.

Mix remaining ingredients in small bowl. Spoon into hollowed bread shell. Cover shell with top of bread; place on cookie sheet.

Bake at 350°F for 1 hour. Serve with bread pieces and crackers.

To reheat, microwave filled bread shell with top on HIGH 1 to 2 minutes or until thoroughly heated, stirring once.

One Bowl Chocolate *Fudge*

(Photo on page 51.)

Prep time: 15 minutes plus refrigerating

Makes 4 dozen squares

2 packages (8 squares *each*) BAKER'S Semi-Sweet Baking Chocolate
1 can (14 ounces) sweetened condensed milk
2 teaspoons vanilla
1 cup chopped nuts *or* toasted BAKER'S ANGEL FLAKE Coconut

Microwave chocolate and milk in microwavable bowl on HIGH 2 minutes or until chocolate is almost melted, stirring halfway through heating time. Stir until chocolate is completely melted.

Stir in vanilla and nuts. Spread in foil-lined 8-inch square pan.

Refrigerate 2 hours or until firm. Cut into squares.

Double Chocolate Orange Nut Fudge: Prepare as directed, using 1 cup toasted chopped walnuts for nuts. Spread in pan. Before refrigerating fudge, melt 1 package (6 squares) BAKER'S Premium White Baking Chocolate as directed on package. Stir in additional ½ cup sweetened condensed milk and 1 teaspoon grated orange peel. Spread over fudge in pan.

Chocolate Berry Dessert Cups

Prep time: 15 minutes plus refrigerating

Makes 8 servings

2½ cups cold milk

2 packages (4-serving size *each*)
JELL-O Chocolate Flavor Instant
Pudding & Pie Filling

2 cups thawed COOL WHIP Whipped
Topping

1 package (10¾ ounces) marble pound
cake, cut into 1-inch cubes

2 cups raspberries *or* strawberries,
hulled, halved

Pour milk into large bowl. Add pudding mixes. Beat with wire whisk 1 minute. (Mixture will be thick.) Immediately stir in whipped topping.

Spoon ⅓ of the pudding mixture into 8 dessert dishes. Top with cake cubes. Add remaining pudding mixture.

Refrigerate 2 hours or until set. Just before serving, top with raspberries. Garnish with fresh mint leaves. Store leftover dessert in refrigerator.

GOOD TO THE LAST DROP® Coffee

Brewing the perfect cup of coffee is easy when you remember five basic rules:

1. Always start with cold water.

2. Be precise with measuring. Use one rounded tablespoon for each six fluid ounces.

3. Serve it freshly brewed.

4. Store ground coffee in a tightly sealed container in your refrigerator or freezer.

5. Clean your coffeemaker regularly.

Chocolate Berry
Dessert Cups (recipe
opposite page)

One Bowl
Chocolate Fudge
(recipe, page 49)

Double Chocolate
Orange Nut Fudge
(recipe, page 49)

Eggnog Coffee
(recipe opposite page)

Holiday Brunch

Eggnog Coffee
Easy Italian Dip
Easy Cheesy Spinach Bake
Chicken Caesar Salad
Parmesan Breadstick Candy Canes
Berry Parfaits

Eggnog Coffee

Prep time: 10 minutes

Makes 5 servings

¼	cup MAXWELL HOUSE Coffee, any variety
¼	teaspoon ground nutmeg
2	tablespoons sugar
2½	cups cold water
1	cup hot eggnog
	Thawed COOL WHIP Whipped Topping

Place coffee and nutmeg in brew basket of coffee maker. Place sugar in empty pot of coffee maker. Prepare coffee with cold water. When brewing is complete, stir in hot eggnog. Serve immediately. Top each serving with whipped topping. Sprinkle with additional nutmeg.

Easy Italian Dip

Prep time: 5 minutes plus refrigerating

Makes 2 cups

1	container (16 ounces) BREAKSTONE'S or KNUDSEN Sour Cream
1	envelope GOOD SEASONS Gourmet Parmesan Italian or Italian Salad Dressing Mix

Mix sour cream and salad dressing mix. Stir in 1 other suggested ingredient, if desired. Cover. Refrigerate. Garnish with fresh basil leaves. Serve with assorted cut-up vegetables or breadsticks.

Suggested ingredients: Stir in any 1 of the following:

- ½ cup chopped roasted red pepper
- 1 teaspoon jarred roasted minced garlic
- 1 can (8½ ounces) artichoke hearts, drained, finely chopped

Easy Cheesy *Spinach* Bake

Prep time: 10 minutes   Baking time: 40 minutes

Makes 8 servings

1   **container (16 ounces) BREAKSTONE'S *or* KNUDSEN Cottage Cheese**

1   **package (10 ounces) frozen chopped spinach, thawed, well drained**

1   **cup KRAFT Shredded Low-Moisture Part-Skim Mozzarella Cheese**

½   **cup OSCAR MAYER Real Bacon Bits**

½   **cup sliced green onions**

4   **eggs, beaten**

Mix all ingredients.

Pour into greased 9-inch pie plate.

Bake at 350°F for 40 minutes or until center is set. Cut into wedges. Garnish each serving with red pepper slivers.

Variation: Prepare as directed. Pour into greased 13×9-inch baking dish. Bake at 350°F for 30 minutes or until center is set. Cut into squares. Makes 10 servings.

Chicken Caesar Salad

Prep time: 15 minutes   Cooking time: 8 minutes

Makes 4 servings

¾ **cup KRAFT Classic Caesar Dressing or KRAFT Caesar Italian Dressing, divided**

1 **pound boneless skinless chicken breasts, cut into strips**

1 **package (10 ounces) mixed or romaine salad greens**

1 **cup seasoned croutons**

½ **cup (2 ounces) KRAFT Shredded or 100% Grated Parmesan Cheese**

Heat ¼ cup of the dressing in skillet on medium-high heat. Add chicken; cook and stir 8 minutes or until cooked through.

Toss greens, croutons, cheese and chicken in large salad bowl with remaining ½ cup dressing.

Serve with fresh lemon wedges and fresh ground pepper, if desired.

Variation: Prepare as directed, substituting KRAFT FREE Classic Caesar Fat Free Dressing or KRAFT FREE Caesar Italian Fat Free Dressing for regular dressing.

Parmesan Breadstick *Candy Canes*

Prep time: 10 minutes   Baking time: 18 minutes

Makes 16

1   can (11 ounces) refrigerated soft
    breadsticks
3   tablespoons butter *or* margarine,
    melted
¾   cup (3 ounces) KRAFT 100% Grated
    Parmesan Cheese

Separate dough; cut each piece in half to make 16 breadsticks. Dip in butter; coat with cheese.

Twist and shape into candy cane shapes on ungreased cookie sheet.

Bake at 350°F for 14 to 18 minutes or until golden brown.

Seasoned Breadstick Candy Canes: Prepare as directed, substituting PARM PLUS! Seasoning Blend for KRAFT 100% Grated Parmesan Cheese.

Berry Parfaits

Prep time: 15 minutes   Refrigerating time: 5¼ hours

Makes 8 servings

1½   **cups boiling water**
1   **package (6 ounces) or 2 packages
     (3 ounces *each*) JELL-O Sparkling Wild
     Berry Flavor Gelatin Dessert**
2   **cups cold raspberry *or* strawberry
     seltzer**
1   **cup raspberries *or* sliced strawberries**
1   **cup thawed COOL WHIP Whipped
     Topping**

Stir boiling water into gelatin in large bowl at least 2 minutes until completely dissolved. Stir in cold seltzer. Reserve 1 cup at room temperature. Refrigerate remaining gelatin 1¼ hours or until thickened. (Spoon drawn through leaves definite impression.)

Stir berries into thickened gelatin. Divide among 8 dessert glasses. Stir whipped topping into reserved 1 cup gelatin with wire whisk until smooth. Spoon over gelatin in glasses.

Refrigerate 4 hours or until firm. Garnish with additional whipped topping, berries and fresh mint leaves. Store leftover dessert in refrigerator.

Note: If desired, recipe can be prepared in 2-quart serving bowl.

Hanukkah Gathering

Pickle Rye Toppers
Grilled fish with SEVEN SEAS® Simply Marinade
Latkes with Sour Cream
Noodle Kugel, Miniature Cheesecakes
and/or Coconut Chocolate Jumbles

Pickle Rye Toppers

**Rye bread, cut into festive shapes *or*
cocktail party rye breads**
**PHILADELPHIA FLAVORS Chive & Onion
Cream Cheese**
**CLAUSSEN Whole Deli Style Hearty
Garlic Pickles, thinly sliced**
**Red pepper, thinly sliced into small
strips**
**Green and yellow pepper, finely
chopped**

Spread breads with cream cheese.

Top each with pickles and red
pepper strips. Sprinkle with green and
yellow pepper.

Noodle Kugel
(recipe, page 61)

Latkes with Sour
Cream (tip, page 61)

SEVEN SEAS® *Simply* Marinade

Prep time: 5 minutes plus marinating   Grilling time or Broiling time: 18 minutes

Makes 4 to 6 servings

1   cup SEVEN SEAS VIVA Italian Dressing, divided
1½ pounds fish and vegetables

Pour ¾ cup of the dressing over fish and vegetables; cover.

Refrigerate 30 minutes to 1 hour to marinate. Drain; discard dressing.

Place fish and vegetables on greased grill over medium coals or on rack of broiler pan 4 to 6 inches from heat. Grill or broil to desired doneness, turning and brushing with remaining ¼ cup dressing. Garnish with fresh tarragon and dill flower.

Variation: Prepare as directed, substituting 1 pound boneless skinless chicken breasts or beef steak for fish and vegetables. Marinate chicken 1 to 4 hours or overnight, or marinate beef 4 hours or overnight.

Noodle Kugel

(Photo on page 59.)

Prep time: 15 minutes   Baking time: 1 hour plus cooling

Makes 12 servings

1   **container (16 ounces) BREAKSTONE'S *or* KNUDSEN Cottage Cheese**
1   **container (16 ounces) BREAKSTONE'S *or* KNUDSEN Sour Cream**
1   **cup sugar**
5   **eggs, beaten**
½   **cup (1 stick) butter *or* margarine, melted**
1   **tablespoon vanilla**
1   **package (12 ounces) broad egg noodles, cooked, rinsed and drained**
   Cinnamon sugar

Mix all ingredients except noodles and cinnamon sugar until well blended. Stir in noodles. Pour into 13×9-inch baking dish; sprinkle with cinnamon sugar.

Bake at 350°F for 1 hour. Cool at least 10 minutes; cut into squares. Serve warm.

Note: To serve as a side dish, reduce sugar to ½ cup.

Noodle Kugel with Fruit: Prepare kugel as directed, stirring in any one of the following with noodles: ½ cup dried cherries, ½ cup dried cranberries, 1 cup raisins, 2 large apples, peeled, chopped or 1 can (8 ounces) crushed pineapple, drained.

Crunch Topped Noodle Kugel: Prepare kugel as directed. Mix 1 cup coarsely crushed corn flakes and 2 tablespoons melted butter *or* margarine. Sprinkle over kugel before baking.

Latkes with Sour Cream

Have your potato pancakes ready 30 minutes ahead of your desired serving time so you can be free to join the festivities or tend to other last-minute details of your party. Simply keep your latkes warm in a 250°F oven. When it comes time to serve your potato latkes, top them with BREAKSTONE'S or KNUDSEN Sour Cream.

Miniature Cheesecakes (recipe opposite page)

Coconut Chocolate Jumbles (recipe, page 64)

Miniature Cheesecakes

(Photo on opposite page and front cover.)

Prep time: 15 minutes plus refrigerating

Makes 12

1 **package (11.1 ounces) JELL-O No Bake Real Cheesecake**

2 **tablespoons sugar**

⅓ **cup butter *or* margarine, melted**

1½ **cups cold milk**

BAKER'S Semi-Sweet Baking Chocolate Squares, melted (optional)

Mix Crumbs, sugar and butter thoroughly with fork in medium bowl until crumbs are well moistened. Press onto bottoms of 12 paper-lined muffin cups.

Beat milk and Filling Mix with electric mixer on low speed until blended. Beat on medium speed 3 minutes. (Filling will be thick.) Spoon over crumb mixture in muffin cups.

Refrigerate at least 1 hour or until ready to serve. Drizzle with melted chocolate. Garnish with assorted fruit and fresh mint leaves. Store leftover cheesecakes in refrigerator.

Coconut Chocolate *Jumbles*

(Photo on page 62.)

Prep time: 15 minutes   Baking time: 12 minutes

Makes about 3 dozen

½ **cup (1 stick) butter *or* margarine**
¾ **cup sugar**
1 **egg**
1 **cup flour**
1 **teaspoon baking soda**
¼ **teaspoon salt**
6 **squares BAKER'S Semi-Sweet Baking Chocolate, chopped**
1 **package (7 ounces) BAKER'S ANGEL FLAKE Coconut (2⅔ cups)**
1 **cup chopped walnuts, toasted**

Beat butter and sugar in large bowl with electric mixer on medium speed until light and fluffy. Beat in egg. Mix in flour, baking soda and salt. Stir in chocolate, coconut and walnuts.

Drop by rounded tablespoonfuls, 1½ inches apart, onto ungreased cookie sheets.

Bake at 350°F for 10 to 12 minutes or until golden brown. Cool for 2 to 3 minutes; remove from cookie sheets. Cool on wire racks. Store in tightly covered container.

Toasting Nuts

Toasting gives nuts a deeper, richer flavor and helps them stay crisp when tossed in salads. Here's how to toast nuts: Spread them in a single layer in a shallow baking pan. Bake at 350°F for 5 to 10 minutes or until golden brown. Watch the nuts carefully and stir them once or twice so they don't burn.

Kwanzaa Dinner

Simple Smokie Squares
Crispy Chicken with Honey Dipping Sauce
15-Minute Chicken & Rice Dinner
Steamed okra or snap peas
Corn Pudding Bars
Fluffy Pumpkin Cheesecake or Heavenly Chocolate Cake

Simple Smokie Squares

(Photo on page 66.)

Prep time: 10 minutes   Baking time: 12 minutes

Makes about 4 dozen

2   cans (10 ounces *each)* refrigerated pizza crust
1   package (16 ounces) OSCAR MAYER Little Smokies *or* Little Wieners
1   package (8 ounces) KRAFT Shredded Colby & Monterey Jack Cheese

Spray 2 cookie sheets with no stick cooking spray. Unroll each pizza crust onto 1 cookie sheet.

Arrange Little Smokies evenly on each crust; press lightly into crust. Sprinkle each crust with 1 cup of cheese.

Bake at 425°F for 12 minutes or until golden brown. Cut into squares.

Crispy Chicken with
Honey Dipping Sauce
(recipe opposite page)

Simple Smokie Squares
(recipe, page 65)

Crispy Chicken with Honey Dipping Sauce

Prep time: 10 minutes   Baking time: 14 minutes

Makes 8 servings

1   cup KRAFT Mayo: Real *or* Light
     Mayonnaise
¼   cup honey
2   tablespoons Dijon mustard *or* Chinese
     hot mustard
2   tablespoons peanut butter
4   boneless skinless chicken breast halves
     (about 1¼ pounds), cut into strips
1½   cups finely crushed potato chips

Mix mayo, honey, mustard and peanut butter. Remove ½ cup of the mayo mixture; set remaining aside.

Brush chicken with ½ cup of the mayo mixture; coat with crushed chips. Place on greased cookie sheet.

Bake at 425°F for 7 to 9 minutes. Turn. Bake an additional 4 to 5 minutes or until lightly browned. Serve with remaining mayo mixture as dipping sauce. Garnish with fresh chives.

Memorable Meals

Some of the fondest memories are those made around a table, enjoying good food and conversation with friends and family. To savor those special moments always, make a mealtime memory book. When everyone is seated at the table, take pictures of the setting from several angles. (Be sure someone else takes a picture that includes you!) When you get your prints, date them and place them in a scrapbook. Write a few notes about who was there, what was served and the goings-on during the party. As you page through this book in years to come, you'll recall the flavors of the food and hear the laughter of your guests with clarity.

15-Minute Chicken & Rice Dinner

Prep/cooking time: 15 minutes

Makes 4 servings

1	tablespoon oil*
4	small boneless skinless chicken breast halves (about 1 pound)
1½	cups water
1	can (10¾ ounces) condensed cream of chicken soup
⅛ to ¼	teaspoon *each* paprika and pepper (optional)
2	cups MINUTE White Rice, uncooked
2	cups fresh *or* frozen broccoli flowerets, thawed (optional)

Heat oil in large nonstick skillet on medium-high heat. Add chicken; cover. Cook 4 minutes on each side or until cooked through. Remove from skillet.

Add water, soup and seasonings to skillet; stir. Bring to boil. Stir in rice and broccoli. Top with chicken; cover. Cook on low heat 5 minutes. Garnish with fresh oregano.

*Note: Increase oil to 2 tablespoons if using regular skillet.

Sharing a Favorite Family Recipe

Touch the taste buds as well as the heart by framing a photograph of your mother, grandmother or aunt along with a nicely handwritten or calligraphic copy of her most beloved recipe. Give the gift to a daughter, son, sister, brother or grandchild. It's a wonderful way to make a cherished recipe part of your family lore.

Corn Pudding Bars
(recipe, page 70)

15-Minute Chicken &
Rice Dinner (recipe
opposite page)

Corn Pudding Bars

(Photo on page 69.)

Prep time: 10 minutes   Baking time: 40 minutes

Makes 12 servings

1   **can (15½ ounces) whole kernel corn, drained**
1   **can (15 ounces) cream-style corn**
1   **package (8½ ounces) corn muffin mix**
1   **cup BREAKSTONE'S *or* KNUDSEN Sour Cream**
3   **eggs**
¼   **cup (½ stick) butter *or* margarine, melted**

Mix all ingredients.

Spoon into 13×9-inch baking dish sprayed with no stick cooking spray.

Bake at 375°F for 35 to 40 minutes. Cut into bars. Serve with additional butter.

Calico Corn Pudding Bars: Prepare as directed, adding ¼ cup *each* finely chopped red pepper and green onions.

Note: Recipe can be baked in 9-inch square baking dish. Increase baking time to 55 to 60 minutes. Makes 9 servings.

Fluffy *Pumpkin* Cheesecake
(Photo on page 73.)

Prep time: 15 minutes plus refrigerating

Makes 8 servings

1   **package (8 ounces) PHILADELPHIA Cream
    Cheese, softened**
1   **cup canned pumpkin**
½   **cup sugar**
½   **teaspoon pumpkin pie spice**
1   **tub (8 ounces) COOL WHIP Whipped
    Topping, thawed**
1   **prepared graham cracker crumb crust
    (6 ounce *or* 9 inch)**

Beat cream cheese, pumpkin, sugar and pumpkin pie spice in large bowl with wire whisk or electric mixer on high speed until smooth. Gently stir in whipped topping. Spoon into crust.

Refrigerate 3 hours or until set. Garnish with additional whipped topping, sliced kiwi and curled orange peel. Sprinkle with ground cinnamon, if desired. Store leftover cheesecake in refrigerator.

Heavenly Chocolate Cake

Prep time: 10 minutes   Baking time: 35 minutes plus cooling

Makes 12 servings

Cake
- 1 package (2-layer size) chocolate cake mix (do not use pudding-in-the-mix variety)
- ½ cup unsweetened cocoa
- 3 eggs
- 1⅓ cups water
- 1 cup MIRACLE WHIP Salad Dressing

Frosting
- 1 package (8 ounces) PHILADELPHIA Cream Cheese, softened
- 2 tablespoons milk
- 1 teaspoon vanilla
- 5 cups sifted powdered sugar
- ½ cup unsweetened cocoa

Cake: Grease and flour 2 (9-inch) round cake pans. Line bottoms of pans with wax paper. Stir cake mix and cocoa in large mixing bowl; add remaining ingredients. Beat with electric mixer on low speed 30 seconds, scraping bowl frequently. Beat with electric mixer on medium speed 2 minutes. Pour batter into prepared pans.

Bake at 350°F for 30 to 35 minutes or until toothpick inserted in center comes out clean. Cool 10 minutes; remove from pans. Immediately remove wax paper. Cool completely on wire racks.

Frosting: Beat cream cheese, milk and vanilla with electric mixer on medium speed until well blended. Mix powdered sugar and cocoa. Gradually add to cream cheese mixture, beating well after each addition. Fill and frost layers. Garnish with unsweetened cocoa and chocolate twigs.

Heavenly Mint Chocolate Cake (photo on front cover)

Looking for an impressive dessert that's easy to make? Prepare the luscious cake shown on the front cover. Start by baking the Heavenly Chocolate Cake (recipe above). Instead of making the frosting, stir green food coloring into 1 cup ready-to-spread vanilla frosting; spread over top of 1 cake layer. Top with second cake layer. Frost top and side of cake with 1 container (16 ounces) ready-to-spread chocolate frosting. Garnish with chopped chocolate mint candies, raspberries and mint leaves.

Heavenly Chocolate
Cake (recipe
opposite page)

Fluffy Pumpkin
Cheesecake (recipe,
page 71)

Cheesy Little Link
Snack Wraps (recipe
opposite page)

CRACKER BARREL®
on Crackers (recipe
opposite page)

New Year's Gala

Cheesy Little Link Snack Wraps
CRACKER BARREL® on Crackers
Antipasto
Carbonara Appetizers
VELVEETA® Salsa Dip
Caramel Pecan Brownies
Tempting Raspberry Tarts

Cheesy Little Link Snack Wraps

Prep time: 10 minutes   Baking time: 12 minutes

Makes 24

6 **KRAFT Singles Process Cheese Food**
1 **can (8 ounces) refrigerated crescent dinner rolls**
24 **OSCAR MAYER Little Smokies *or* Little Wieners**

Cut each process cheese food slice into 4 strips; cut strips in half.

Separate dough into triangles; cut into thirds. Top each dough piece with 2 process cheese food pieces and Little Smokie. Roll up. Place on ungreased cookie sheet.

Bake at 375°F for 12 minutes or until golden brown.

CRACKER BARREL® on *Crackers*

Prep time: 15 minutes

Makes 20 snacks

20 **assorted crackers**
1 **package (10 ounces) CRACKER BARREL Extra Sharp Natural Cheddar Cheese, sliced**
20 **slices fresh strawberries**

Top crackers with cheese slices and strawberry slices.

Antipasto

Prep time: 15 minutes plus marinating

Makes 8 to 10 servings

1 **bottle (8 ounces) SEVEN SEAS VIVA Italian Dressing**

1 **package (3 ounces) OSCAR MAYER Pepperoni Slices**

1 **can (14 ounces) artichoke hearts, drained, quartered**

1 **cup halved cherry tomatoes**

1 **cup pitted ripe olives**

10 **pepperoncini**

4 **ounces KRAFT Low-Moisture Part-Skim Mozzarella Cheese, cut into ¼-inch sticks**

Pour dressing over pepperoni, artichoke hearts, tomatoes, olives and pepperoncini;

cover. Refrigerate overnight to marinate. Drain, reserving dressing.

Toss pepperoni, vegetables and cheese with reserved dressing. Spoon onto serving platter.

Arranged Antipasto: Marinate and drain pepperoni and vegetables as directed. Arrange pepperoni, vegetables and cheese on platter. Serve with reserved dressing.

Tossed Antipasto Salad: Marinate pepperoni and vegetables as directed. Toss pepperoni, vegetables, cheese and 1 package (10 ounces) salad greens. Makes 4 servings.

Carbonara Appetizers

Prep time: 15 minutes   Baking time: 8 minutes

Makes 6 servings

1   **Italian bread shell (6 inch)**
¼   **cup DI GIORNO Alfredo Sauce**
2   **slices OSCAR MAYER Bacon, crisply cooked, crumbled**
3   **tablespoons chopped red onion**
2   **teaspoons chopped fresh parsley**
2   **teaspoons KRAFT 100% Grated Parmesan Cheese**

Spread bread shell with sauce; layer with remaining ingredients.

Bake on ungreased cookie sheet at 450°F for 8 minutes or until bread shell is crisp and thoroughly heated. Cut into wedges.

Time to Party

The new year is the perfect time to gather family and friends, to celebrate last year's high points and to plan for the upcoming year. Make your New Year's party casual and fun with foods that work well for potluck sharing and nibbling. To assure that the party is easy on the hostess, follow these hints:

• Include warm buffet snack foods that are easy to pick up and eat in one or two bites.

• Dips are great for parties because one dish serves so many. Keep warm dips warm in an electric crockery cooker or serve them in a microwavable casserole that you can pop back into the microwave oven to reheat. For cold dips, serve a variety of KRAFT Dips, such as French onion, blue cheese or nacho cheese.

• Look for dippers with flair. Include different colors and shapes of chips and crackers and serve platters of cut-up vegetables.

• Instead of setting all the food on the buffet table, spread some easy-to-nibble snacks around the room.

• Remember the folks with a sweet tooth by including one or two desserts in your party fare.

VELVEETA® *Salsa Dip*

Prep time: 5 minutes   Microwave time: 5 minutes

Makes 3 cups

**1   pound (16 ounces) VELVEETA Pasteurized
     Prepared Cheese Product, cut up**
**1   cup TACO BELL HOME ORIGINALS Thick 'N
     Chunky Salsa**

Microwave prepared cheese product and salsa in 1½-quart microwavable bowl on HIGH 5 minutes or until prepared cheese product is melted, stirring after 3 minutes.

Serve hot with tortilla chips and pepper strips. Garnish with red and green pepper cutouts.

Caramel Pecan Brownies

Prep time: 20 minutes   Baking time: 55 minutes

Makes 24

4 squares BAKER'S Unsweetened Baking Chocolate

¾ cup (1½ sticks) butter *or* margarine

2 cups sugar

4 eggs

1 cup flour

1 package (14 ounces) caramels, unwrapped

⅓ cup heavy *or* whipping cream

2 cups pecan *or* walnut halves, divided

Line 13×9-inch baking pan or dish with foil extending over edges to form handles. Generously grease foil. Heat oven to 350°F (325°F for glass baking dish).

Microwave chocolate and butter in large microwavable bowl on HIGH 2 minutes or until butter is melted. Stir until chocolate is completely melted. Stir sugar into chocolate until well blended. Mix in eggs. Stir in flour until well blended. Spread ½ of the brownie batter in prepared pan.

Bake for 25 minutes or until brownie batter is firm to the touch.

Meanwhile, microwave caramels and cream in microwavable bowl on HIGH

2 minutes or until caramels begin to melt. Stir until smooth. Stir in 1 cup of the pecan halves. Gently spread caramel mixture over baked brownie batter in pan. Pour remaining unbaked brownie batter evenly over caramel mixture; sprinkle with remaining 1 cup pecan halves. (Some caramel mixture may peek through.)

Bake an additional 30 minutes or until brownies feel firm to the touch. Cool in pan. Gently run knife around edges of pan to loosen brownies from sides. Lift from pan using foil as handles. Cut into squares.

Caramel Chocolate Chip Brownies: Prepare as directed, except sprinkle unbaked caramel mixture in pan with 1 package (12 ounces) BAKER'S Semi-Sweet Real Chocolate Chips. Add remaining brownie batter and nuts. Bake an additional 30 minutes as directed.

Tempting Raspberry Tarts

Prep time: 10 minutes plus refrigerating

Makes 12 servings

¼ **cup honey**
1 **package (8 ounces) PHILADELPHIA Cream Cheese, softened**
1 **package (10 ounces) frozen red raspberries in light syrup, partially thawed, undrained**
1 **cup sliced banana**
2 **cups miniature marshmallows**
1¾ **cups thawed COOL WHIP Whipped Topping**
2 **packages (4 ounces *each*) graham cracker tart shells (12 shells)**

Add honey to cream cheese, mixing until well blended.

Stir in fruits. Gently stir in marshmallows and whipped topping.

Pour into shells. Refrigerate several hours or overnight. Garnish with fresh raspberries, fresh mint leaves and additional marshmallows.

Tempting Strawberry Tarts: Prepare as directed, substituting 1 package (10 ounces) frozen strawberry halves in light syrup for raspberries.

Savory Sub
Sandwich
(recipe, page 82)

Big Bowl Bash

Savory Sub Sandwich or Super Sub Sandwich
Super Stack Parmesan Pizza
The Original Munch Mix
VELVEETA® Cheesy Chili Dip
Time-Out Munchies
Sparkling Punch

Super Sub Sandwich

Prep time: 10 minutes

Makes 8 servings

2 cups broccoli slaw *or* coleslaw blend

1 cup MIRACLE WHIP Salad Dressing *or* KRAFT Mayo Real Mayonnaise, divided

1 loaf (about 16 ounces) French bread, cut in half lengthwise

1 package (12 ounces) OSCAR MAYER Smoked Cooked Ham

1 package (8 ounces) OSCAR MAYER Bologna

8 KRAFT Singles Process Cheese Food

2 tomatoes, sliced

Mix slaw and ½ cup of the salad dressing.

Spread bread halves with remaining salad dressing.

Layer bottom half of bread with slaw mixture and remaining ingredients. Cover with top half of bread.

Savory Sub Sandwich: (Photo on page 81.) Prepare Super Sub Sandwich as directed, adding 6 slices OSCAR MAYER Center Cut Bacon, crisply cooked, to sandwich.

Super Combo Sub: Prepare Super Sub Sandwich as directed, substituting 1 package (16 ounces) OSCAR MAYER Combo Pack Meats for bologna and ham.

Family Favorite Super Sub: Prepare Super Sub Sandwich as directed, substituting any of your family's favorite sandwich toppings, such as roasted red pepper strips, tri-color pepper rings or red onion slices.

Mini Sub: Prepare Super Sub Sandwich as directed, using 1 loaf (8 ounces) mini French bread and dividing all other ingredient amounts in half.

The Original *Munch* Mix

Prep time: 5 minutes   Baking time: 35 minutes

Makes about 8 cups

4 cups **POST SPOON SIZE** Shredded Wheat
   Cereal
2 cups popped popcorn
1 cup small pretzels
1 cup mixed nuts *or* peanuts
1 envelope **GOOD SEASONS** Italian Salad
   Dressing Mix
¼ cup (½ stick) margarine, melted
2 tablespoons Worcestershire sauce
¼ teaspoon garlic powder (optional)

Place cereal, popcorn, pretzels and nuts in 15×10×1-inch baking pan. Sprinkle evenly with salad dressing mix.

Mix margarine, Worcestershire sauce and garlic powder. Drizzle evenly over cereal mixture; toss to coat.

Bake at 300°F for 30 to 35 minutes or until crisp, stirring halfway through baking time. Cool. Store in tightly covered container.

VELVEETA® Cheesy
Chili Dip (recipe
opposite page)

CHEEZ WHIZ over
tortilla chips (tip
opposite page)

VELVEETA® Cheesy *Chili Dip*

Prep time: 5 minutes   Microwave time: 5 minutes

Makes 3¾ cups

**1   pound (16 ounces) VELVEETA Pasteurized
     Prepared Cheese Product, cut up**
1   can (15 ounces) chili

Microwave prepared cheese product and chili in 2-quart microwavable bowl on HIGH 5 minutes or until prepared cheese product is melted, stirring after 3 minutes.

Serve hot with tortilla chips or red, green and/or yellow pepper strips.

Time-Out Munchies

Set out an assortment of easy-to-fix munchies for guests to snack on while they watch the big game. Start with any or all of these ideas:

• **Pour heated CHEEZ WHIZ** Pasteurized Process Cheese Sauce onto tortilla chips. Top with jalapeño pepper slices. Serve along with TACO BELL HOME ORIGINALS Thick 'N Chunky Salsa.

• **Spread PHILADELPHIA FLAVORS** Garden Vegetable Cream Cheese onto crackers. Garnish with chopped red pepper and snipped fresh chives.

• **Team sliced CRACKER BARREL** Extra Sharp Natural Cheddar Cheese with assorted crackers.

• **Serve your favorite KRAFT Dips** with potato or tortilla chips, pretzels or assorted cut-up vegetables.

Super Stack *Parmesan* Pizza

Prep time: 5 minutes   Baking time: 30 minutes

Makes 8 to 12 servings

2 frozen **TOMBSTONE Pepperoni Pizzas**
⅔ cup **KRAFT 100% Grated Parmesan Cheese**
   Thinly sliced onion

Remove pizzas from overwrap and cardboard. Top each pizza with cheese and onion.

Stack pizzas, one on top of the other; place directly on oven rack in second-from-bottom position (5 to 7 inches from bottom of oven).

Bake at 400°F for 25 to 30 minutes or until cheese is melted and edges are golden brown.

Sparkling Punch

Prep time: 5 minutes

Makes 6 to 10 servings

1   cup **TANG** Brand Orange Flavor Drink Mix

1½ cups pineapple juice *or* cranberry juice cocktail

1   bottle (1 liter) chilled ginger ale *or* club soda
    Ice cubes

Dissolve drink mix in pineapple juice in pitcher or punch bowl.

Stir in ginger ale and ice cubes. Garnish with orange slices.

Merry Cherry
Holiday Dessert
(recipe, page 100)

New York
Cheesecake (recipe,
page 90)

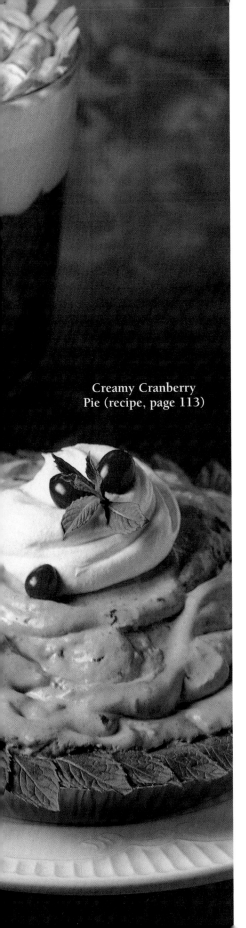

Creamy Cranberry Pie (recipe, page 113)

VISIONS OF DECADENT DESSERTS

Since this is the season for sugar plums, sharing the goodness of homemade desserts at your holiday happenings is only natural. Now you can create dozens of popular holiday flavors even if you're short on time, thanks to this merry assortment of cakes, pies, cheesecakes and other tempting desserts.

New York Cheesecake

(Photo on pages 88–89.)

Prep time: 15 minutes plus refrigerating Baking time: 1 hour 10 minutes

Makes 14 servings

1 **cup graham cracker crumbs**
3 **tablespoons sugar**
3 **tablespoons butter *or* margarine,
    melted**
5 **packages (8 ounces *each*) PHILADELPHIA
    Cream Cheese, softened**
1 **cup sugar**
3 **tablespoons flour**
1 **tablespoon vanilla**
3 **eggs**
1 **cup BREAKSTONE'S *or* KNUDSEN Sour
    Cream**
1 **can (21 ounces) cherry pie filling**

Mix crumbs, 3 tablespoons sugar and butter; press onto bottom of 9-inch springform pan. Bake at 350°F for 10 minutes.

Mix cream cheese, 1 cup sugar, flour and vanilla with electric mixer on medium speed until well blended. Add eggs, 1 at a time, mixing on low speed after each addition, just until blended. Blend in sour cream. Pour over crust.

Bake 1 hour and 5 minutes to 1 hour and 10 minutes or until center is almost set. Run small knife or metal spatula around rim of pan to loosen cake; cool before removing rim of pan. Refrigerate 4 hours or overnight. Top with pie filling. Garnish with piped cream cheese. Store leftover cheesecake in refrigerator.

15% off

ny apparel purchase

avings off regular, sale and clearance prices
ply to merchandise only. Not valid on
ceptional Values, Special Purchases, Great
ice Items, Lands' End® merchandise, Levi's
ns, sears.com, Sears Auctions on ebay®,
talog orders and Gift Cards. One coupon per
rchase. Void if copied, transferred and where
hibited by law. Any other use constitutes
ud. Cash value 1/20 cent. In the event of a
urn, coupon savings may be deducted from
r refund.

004 Sears Brands, LLC.

sfaction Guaranteed or Your Money Back℠

es Associate: please collect this coupon. If
ble to scan, manually enter the coupon
ber.

d November 21 through
ember 24, 2004 in U.S.A.
. May not be used with
other coupon.

R 588034515

3-STEP™ Luscious *Lemon* Cheesecake

Prep time: 10 minutes   Baking time: 40 minutes

Makes 8 servings

s *each*) **PHILADELPHIA**
ftened

mon juice
non peel

m cracker crumb
9 inch)

1. Mix cream cheese, sugar, juice, peel and vanilla with electric mixer on medium speed until well blended. Add eggs; mix until blended.

2. Pour into crust.

3. Bake at 350°F for 40 minutes or until center is almost set. Cool. Refrigerate 3 hours or overnight. Garnish with fresh raspberries, lemon slices and fresh mint.

Variations:

For a fruit-topped cheesecake, omit juice and peel. Top refrigerated cheesecake with 2 cups sliced assorted fresh fruit.

For a lower fat version, substitute PHILADELPHIA Neufchâtel Cheese, ⅓ Less Fat than Cream Cheese, for regular cream cheese.

White Chocolate Cheesecake

Prep time: 15 minutes plus refrigerating

Makes 8 servings

1   **package (11.1 ounces) JELL-O No Bake Real Cheesecake**

2   **tablespoons sugar**

⅓   **cup butter *or* margarine, melted**

1½ **cups cold milk**

1   **package (6 squares) BAKER'S Premium White Baking Chocolate, melted**

Mix Crumbs, sugar and butter thoroughly with fork in 9-inch pie plate until crumbs are well moistened. Press firmly against sides of pie plate first, using fingers or large spoon to shape edge. Press remaining crumbs firmly onto bottom of pie plate using measuring cup.

Beat milk and Filling Mix with electric mixer on low speed until blended. Beat on medium speed 3 minutes. (Filling will be thick.) Stir in melted white chocolate. Spoon into crust.

Refrigerate at least 1 hour or until ready to serve. Garnish with thawed COOL WHIP Whipped Topping and fruit-shape marzipan or other candies. Store leftover cheesecake in refrigerator.

PHILADELPHIA® *No-Bake* Cheesecake

Prep time: 10 minutes plus refrigerating

Makes 8 servings

1   **package (8 ounces) PHILADELPHIA Cream Cheese, softened**
⅓ **cup sugar**
1   **tub (8 ounces) COOL WHIP Whipped Topping, thawed**
1   **prepared graham cracker crumb crust (6 ounce *or* 9 inch)***

Mix cream cheese and sugar with electric mixer on medium speed until well blended. Gently stir in whipped topping.

Spoon into crust. Refrigerate 3 hours or overnight. Top with fresh fruit or cherry pie filling, if desired. Store leftover cheesecake in refrigerator.

***Note:** To transfer a purchased crust to your own pie plate, use kitchen shears to carefully cut foil pan. Then, peel pan from crust and place in pie plate.

Keep on Hand Cheesecake

When you have a little time early in the holiday season, make PHILADELPHIA® No-Bake Cheesecake and freeze it until you need it. To serve the cheesecake, place it in the refrigerator to thaw for about 8 hours. Top with fruit or pie filling just before serving.

Chocolate Cheesecake Bars

Prep time: 15 minutes plus refrigerating or Freezing time: 4 hours

Makes 18 bars

- **1** package (11.1 ounces) JELL-O No Bake Real Cheesecake
- **2** tablespoons sugar
- **⅓** cup butter *or* margarine, melted
- **1½** cups cold milk
- **1** square BAKER'S Semi-Sweet Baking Chocolate, melted
- **½** cup chopped nuts

Line 8-inch square pan with foil, extending over edges to form handles.

Mix Crumbs, sugar and butter with fork in bowl until crumbs are well moistened.

Press firmly onto bottom of pan using measuring cup.

Beat milk and Filling Mix with electric mixer on low speed until blended. Beat on medium speed 3 minutes. (Filling will be thick.) Spread ½ of the filling over crust.

Stir chocolate into remaining filling. Spread over filling in pan. Sprinkle with nuts.

Refrigerate at least 1 hour or freeze 4 hours. Remove from pan; cut into bars. Store leftover bars in refrigerator or freezer.

Chocolate *Candy Bar* Dessert

Prep time: 20 minutes plus refrigerating

Makes 15 to 18 servings

2   **cups chocolate wafer cookie crumbs**
½   **cup sugar, divided**
½   **cup (1 stick) butter *or* margarine,
     melted**
1   **package (8 ounces) PHILADELPHIA Cream
     Cheese, softened**
1   **tub (12 ounces) COOL WHIP Whipped
     Topping, thawed, divided**
1   **cup chopped chocolate-covered candy
     bars**
3   **cups cold milk**
2   **packages (4-serving size *each*) JELL-O
     Chocolate Flavor Instant Pudding &
     Pie Filling**

Mix cookie crumbs, ¼ cup of the sugar and butter in 13×9-inch pan. Press firmly onto bottom of pan. Refrigerate 10 minutes.

Mix cream cheese and remaining ¼ cup sugar in medium bowl with wire whisk until smooth. Gently stir in ½ of the whipped topping. Spread evenly over crust. Sprinkle chopped candy bars over cream cheese layer.

Pour milk into large bowl. Add pudding mixes. Beat with wire whisk 1 minute. Pour over chopped candy bar layer. Let stand 5 minutes or until thickened. Spread remaining whipped topping over pudding layer.

Refrigerate 2 hours or until set. Garnish with additional chopped candy bars. Cut into squares. Store leftover dessert in refrigerator.

Chocolate-Walnut Torte

Prep time: 15 minutes   Baking time: 40 minutes plus cooling

Makes 10 servings

½   cup (1 stick) butter *or* margarine, softened
¾   cup granulated sugar, divided
1   package (8 squares) BAKER'S Semi-Sweet Baking Chocolate, melted, cooled
7   eggs, separated
1½   cups ground walnuts
⅓   cup flour
    Powdered sugar

Beat butter and ½ cup of the granulated sugar with electric mixer on medium speed until light and fluffy. Blend in cooled chocolate. Add egg yolks, 1 at a time, beating well after each addition. Toss walnuts and flour. Stir into butter mixture.

Beat egg whites until foamy. Gradually add remaining ¼ cup granulated sugar, beating until soft peaks form. Stir ¼ of the egg whites into chocolate batter. Fold in remaining egg whites. Spray 9-inch springform pan with no stick cooking spray. Pour batter into springform pan.

Bake at 350°F for 40 minutes or until toothpick inserted in center comes out clean. Cool in pan 10 minutes. Remove rim and cool completely. Sprinkle with powdered sugar. Garnish with additional walnut pieces and fresh mint. Cut into wedges to serve.

Merry Cherry *Holiday* Dessert

(Photo on pages 88–89.)

Prep time: 20 minutes   Refrigerating time: 3¾ hours

Makes 16 servings

1½   **cups boiling water**
  1   **package (8-serving size) *or* 2 packages (4-serving size *each*) JELL-O Cherry Flavor Gelatin Dessert**
1½   **cups cold water**
  1   **can (21 ounces) cherry pie filling**
  4   **cups angel food cake cubes**
  3   **cups cold milk**
  2   **packages (4-serving size *each*) JELL-O Vanilla Flavor Instant Pudding & Pie Filling**
  1   **tub (8 ounces) COOL WHIP Whipped Topping, thawed**

Stir boiling water into gelatin in large bowl at least 2 minutes until completely dissolved. Stir in cold water and cherry pie filling.

Refrigerate about 1 hour or until slightly thickened. (Gelatin is consistency of unbeaten egg whites.) Place cake cubes in 3-quart serving bowl.

Spoon gelatin mixture over cake. Refrigerate 45 minutes or until set but not firm. (Gelatin should stick to finger when touched and should mound.)

Pour milk into large bowl. Add pudding mixes. Beat with wire whisk 1 minute. Gently stir in 2 cups of the whipped topping. Spoon over gelatin mixture in bowl.

Refrigerate 2 hours or until set. Top with remaining whipped topping. Garnish with toasted sliced almonds. Store leftover dessert in refrigerator.

Berry Heaven

Prep time: 15 minutes plus refrigerating

Makes 12 servings

1   **prepared tube angel food cake
     (9- *or* 10-inch)**
½   **cup raspberry *or* strawberry fruit
     spread *or* jam**
1   **tub (8 ounces) COOL WHIP Whipped
     Topping, thawed**

Cut cake horizontally into 3 layers. Place
1 cake layer on serving plate.

Spread ¼ cup of the fruit spread on cake
layer. Top with ½ cup of the whipped
topping. Repeat layers, ending with cake.
Frost top and sides of cake with remaining
whipped topping.

Refrigerate 1 hour or until ready to
serve. Garnish with fresh raspberries
and fresh mint. Store leftover cake in
refrigerator.

Luscious Lemon Poke Cake

Prep time: 20 minutes plus refrigerating

Makes 12 servings

2   **baked 9-inch round white cake layers,
    cooled**
2   **cups boiling water**
1   **package (8-serving size) *or* 2 packages
    (4-serving size *each*) JELL-O Lemon
    Flavor Gelatin Dessert
    Fluffy Lemon Pudding Frosting (recipe
    below)**

Place cake layers, top sides up, in 2 clean 9-inch round cake pans. Pierce cakes with large fork at ½-inch intervals.

Stir boiling water into gelatin in medium bowl 2 minutes until completely dissolved.

Carefully pour 1 cup of the gelatin over 1 cake layer. Pour remaining gelatin over second cake layer.

Refrigerate 3 hours. Dip 1 cake pan in warm water 10 seconds; unmold onto serving plate. Spread top with about 1 cup of the frosting. Unmold second cake layer; carefully place on first cake layer. Frost top and sides of cake with remaining frosting.

Refrigerate at least 1 hour or until ready to serve. Decorate as desired. Store leftover cake in refrigerator.

Fluffy Lemon Pudding *Frosting*

Prep time: 10 minutes

Makes about 4 cups

1   **cup cold milk**
1   **package (4-serving size) JELL-O Lemon
    Flavor Instant Pudding & Pie Filling**
¼   **cup powdered sugar**
1   **tub (8 ounces) COOL WHIP Whipped
    Topping, thawed**

Pour cold milk into medium bowl. Add pudding mix and sugar. Beat with wire whisk 2 minutes. Gently stir in whipped topping. Immediately spread on cake.

Creamy Holiday *Lemon* Cups

Prep time: 15 minutes   Refrigerating time: 5¼ hours

Makes 10 servings

2 cups boiling water

1 package (8-serving size) *or* 2 packages (4-serving size *each*) JELL-O Lemon Flavor Gelatin Dessert

½ cup cold water

1½ cups cold milk

1 package (4-serving size) JELL-O Vanilla Flavor Instant Pudding & Pie Filling

2 teaspoons rum extract

½ teaspoon ground nutmeg

2 cups thawed COOL WHIP Whipped Topping

Stir boiling water into gelatin in large bowl 2 minutes until completely dissolved. Stir in cold water. Cool to room temperature.

Pour milk into another bowl. Add pudding mix. Beat with wire whisk 30 seconds. Immediately stir into cooled gelatin until smooth. Stir in rum extract and nutmeg. Refrigerate about 1¼ hours or until slightly thickened.

Stir in whipped topping with wire whisk until smooth and creamy. Pour into 10 individual dessert dishes or drinking mugs.

Refrigerate 4 hours or until firm. Garnish with additional whipped topping and sprinkle with additional ground nutmeg just before serving. Store leftover desserts in refrigerator.

Pumpkin Rice Pudding

Prep time: 15 minutes   Baking time: 50 minutes

Makes 14 servings

4	**cups milk**
1	**can (16 ounces) pumpkin**
1	**cup MINUTE White Rice, uncooked**
¾	**cup sugar**
1	**teaspoon ground cinnamon**
½	**teaspoon *each* ground ginger and salt**
¼	**teaspoon ground cloves**
2	**eggs**
½	**teaspoon vanilla**

Bring milk, pumpkin, rice, sugar, cinnamon, ginger, salt and cloves to boil in large saucepan, stirring constantly. Reduce heat to low; simmer 5 minutes, stirring occasionally. Remove from heat.

Beat eggs and vanilla in large bowl. Slowly stir in hot pumpkin mixture, blending well after each addition. Pour into greased 2-quart casserole.

Bake at 375°F for 45 to 50 minutes or until set. Cool slightly. Serve warm or refrigerate until ready to serve. Garnish as desired. Store leftover pudding in refrigerator.

All-Time Favorite *Puff Pudding*

Prep time: 15 minutes   Baking time: 1 hour and 15 minutes

Makes 10 servings

1 cup sugar
½ cup (1 stick) butter *or* margarine, softened
4 egg yolks
2 cups milk
½ cup POST GRAPE-NUTS Cereal
¼ cup flour
¼ cup lemon juice
2 teaspoons grated lemon peel
4 egg whites, stiffly beaten

Beat sugar and butter in large bowl with electric mixer on medium speed until light and fluffy. Beat in egg yolks. Stir in milk, cereal, flour, juice and peel. (Mixture will look curdled.) Gently stir in stiffly beaten egg whites. Pour into greased 2-quart baking dish. Place dish in large baking pan. Fill pan with hot water to depth of 1 inch.

Bake at 350°F for 1 hour and 15 minutes or until top is golden brown and begins to pull away from sides of dish. (Pudding will have cake-like layer on top with custard below.) Garnish with citrus slices and peel, fresh mint leaves and whipped topping. Serve warm or cold with cream or whipped topping, if desired. Store leftover pudding in refrigerator.

Variation: For individual puddings, pour mixture into 10 custard cups. Bake 40 minutes.

Fruity Mousse

Prep time: 10 minutes plus refrigerating

Makes 10 servings

1 **package (8 ounces) PHILADELPHIA Neufchâtel Cheese, ⅓ Less Fat than Cream Cheese, softened**
1 **tub CRYSTAL LIGHT Lemon Lime, Pink Lemonade *or* Cranberry Breeze Flavor Low Calorie Soft Drink Mix, divided**
1 **cup skim milk**
3 **drops green *or* red food coloring**
1 **tub (8 ounces) COOL WHIP FREE Whipped Topping, thawed**

Beat Neufchâtel cheese and 1½ teaspoons of the drink mix in large bowl with electric mixer on medium speed until well blended and smooth. Gradually add milk and food coloring, mixing until well blended. Gently stir in whipped topping until well blended. Pour into serving bowl or individual dishes.

Refrigerate 3 hours or until firm. Serve with additional whipped topping and candied or fresh citrus fruit, if desired. Store leftover mousse in refrigerator.

Note: Place remaining drink mix in plastic pitcher. Add 4 cups (1 quart) water; stir to dissolve. Serve over ice.

Easy *Cappuccino* Topping

Prep time: 10 minutes plus refrigerating

Makes 3½ cups

1 envelope MAXWELL HOUSE Cafe
   Cappuccino, any flavor
2 tablespoons hot water
1 tub (8 ounces) COOL WHIP Whipped
   Topping, thawed

Dissolve cappuccino in hot water in large bowl; cool. Gently stir in whipped topping until blended. Store, covered, in refrigerator.

Spoon over fruit, cake, ice cream or hot beverages. Garnish with fresh mint. Store leftover topping in refrigerator.

Creamy *Pudding* Sauce

Prep time: 5 minutes plus standing

Makes 3½ cups

3½ cups cold skim milk
1 package (4-serving size) JELL-O White Chocolate *or* Devil's Food Flavor Fat Free Instant Pudding & Pie Filling

Pour cold milk into medium bowl. Add pudding mix. Beat with wire whisk 1 minute. Let stand 10 minutes or until slightly thickened.

Serve with assorted fresh fruit. Garnish with fresh raspberries, orange peel and fresh mint leaves. Store leftover sauce in refrigerator.

Note: Thin with small amount of additional milk before serving, if desired.

Cookies & Creme Café Pie

Prep time: 15 minutes plus refrigerating or Freezing time: 2 hours

Makes 8 servings

1   package (12.6 ounces) JELL-O No Bake Cookies & Creme Dessert
⅓   cup butter *or* margarine, melted
1⅓   cups cold milk
¼   cup GENERAL FOODS INTERNATIONAL COFFEES, Suisse Mocha Flavor, Vanilla Cafe Flavor *or* Irish Cream Cafe Flavor

Stir Crust Mix and butter thoroughly with spoon in medium bowl until crumbs are well moistened. Press onto bottom and up sides of 9-inch pie plate.

Pour cold milk into large bowl. Add Filling Mix and coffee. Beat with electric mixer on low speed 30 seconds. Beat on high speed 3 minutes. DO NOT UNDERBEAT.

Reserve ½ cup Crushed Cookies. Gently stir remaining crushed cookies into filling until well blended. Spoon mixture into prepared crust. Top with reserved cookies. Refrigerate 4 hours or until firm or freeze 2 hours to serve frozen. Store leftover pie in refrigerator or freezer.

Candy Bar Pie

Prep time: 20 minutes plus refrigerating

Makes 8 servings

4 ounces PHILADELPHIA Cream Cheese, softened

1 tablespoon milk *or* half-and-half

1 tub (12 ounces) COOL WHIP Whipped Topping, thawed, divided

2 packages (2.07 ounces *each*) chocolate-covered caramel peanut nougat bars, chopped

1½ cups cold milk *or* half-and-half

2 packages (4-serving size *each*) JELL-O Chocolate Flavor Instant Pudding & Pie Filling

1 prepared chocolate flavor crumb crust (6 ounce *or* 9 inch)

Mix cream cheese and 1 tablespoon milk in large bowl with wire whisk until smooth. Gently stir in 1½ cups of the whipped topping and chopped candy bars.

Pour 1½ cups cold milk into another large bowl. Add pudding mixes. Beat with wire whisk 1 minute. (Mixture will be thick.) Gently stir in 2 cups of the whipped topping. Spread ½ of the pudding mixture on bottom of crust. Spread cream cheese mixture over pudding mixture in crust. Spread remaining pudding mixture over cream cheese layer.

Refrigerate 4 hours or until set. Pipe remaining whipped topping around edge of pie. Sprinkle with shaved semi-sweet and white chocolate, if desired. Garnish with piped white and dark chocolate swirls. Store leftover pie in refrigerator.

White Chocolate *Devil's Food* Pie

Prep time: 20 minutes plus refrigerating

Makes 8 servings

1½ cups cold skim milk, divided
  1 package (4-serving size) JELL-O Devil's
     Food Flavor Fat Free Instant Pudding
     & Pie Filling
  1 tub (8 ounces) COOL WHIP LITE Whipped
     Topping, thawed
  1 prepared graham cracker crumb crust
     (6 ounce *or* 9 inch)
  1 package (4-serving size) JELL-O White
     Chocolate Flavor Fat Free Instant
     Pudding & Pie Filling

Pour ¾ cup of the cold milk into medium bowl. Add devil's food flavor pudding mix. Beat with wire whisk 1 minute. (Mixture will be thick.) Gently stir in ½ of the whipped topping. Spoon into crust.

Pour remaining ¾ cup cold milk into another medium bowl. Add white chocolate flavor pudding mix. Beat with wire whisk 1 minute. (Mixture will be thick.) Gently stir in remaining whipped topping. Spread over pudding layer in crust.

Refrigerate 4 hours or until set. Garnish with strawberries and chocolate leaves. Sprinkle with unsweetened cocoa, if desired. Store leftover pie in refrigerator.

Creamy Cranberry Pie

(Photo on pages 88–89.)

Prep time: 20 minutes   Refrigerating time: 4½ hours

Makes 8 servings

⅔ **cup boiling water**
1 **package (4-serving size) JELL-O Cranberry Flavor Gelatin Dessert**
½ **cup cold water**
    Ice cubes
1 **tub (8 ounces) COOL WHIP Whipped Topping, thawed**
1 **teaspoon grated orange peel (optional)**
1 **cup whole berry cranberry sauce**
1 **prepared graham cracker crumb crust (6 ounce *or* 9 inch)**

Stir boiling water into gelatin in large bowl at least 2 minutes until completely dissolved. Mix cold water and ice to measure 1 cup. Add to gelatin, stirring until slightly thickened. Remove any remaining ice.

Stir in whipped topping and orange peel with wire whisk until smooth. Gently stir in cranberry sauce. Refrigerate 20 to 30 minutes or until mixture is very thick and will mound. Spoon into crust.

Refrigerate 4 hours or until firm. Garnish with additional whipped topping, fresh mint leaves and fresh cranberries. Store leftover pie in refrigerator.

Tropical *Coconut Cream* Pie

Prep time: 20 minutes plus refrigerating   Baking time: 10 minutes

Makes 8 servings

1½ **cups shortbread cookie crumbs (about 20 cookies)**

1⅔ **cups BAKER'S ANGEL FLAKE Coconut, divided**

⅓ **cup butter *or* margarine, melted**

1 **large banana, sliced**

1½ **cups cold milk**

1 **package (4-serving size) JELL-O Vanilla Flavor Instant Pudding & Pie Filling**

1 **can (8 ounces) crushed pineapple, well drained**

2 **cups thawed COOL WHIP Whipped Topping**
BAKER'S ANGEL FLAKE Coconut, toasted (optional)

Mix cookie crumbs, ⅔ cup of the coconut and butter in medium bowl until well blended. Press mixture evenly onto bottom and up sides of 9-inch pie plate.

Bake at 325°F for 10 minutes or until golden. Cool. Arrange banana slices in crust.

Pour cold milk into large bowl. Add pudding mix. Beat with wire whisk 1 minute. Stir in remaining 1 cup coconut. Spoon over banana slices in crust. Gently stir pineapple into whipped topping. Spread over pudding mixture. Sprinkle with toasted coconut.

Refrigerate 4 hours or until set. Store leftover pie in refrigerator.

Irish Coffee Pie

Prep time: 10 minutes plus refrigerating

Makes 8 servings

2 cups cold milk
1 tablespoon Irish whiskey
1 package (6-serving size) JELL-O Vanilla
   Flavor Instant Pudding & Pie Filling
2 teaspoons MAXWELL HOUSE Instant
   Coffee
1 baked pastry shell *or* graham cracker
   crumb crust (6 ounce *or* 9 inch)

Pour milk and whiskey into large bowl. Add pudding mix and instant coffee. Beat with wire whisk 2 minutes.

Pour mixture into pastry shell.

Refrigerate 4 hours or until set. Garnish with whipped topping and sprinkle with cinnamon or toasted coconut. Store leftover pie in refrigerator.

Double Layer Pumpkin Pie

Prep time: 20 minutes plus refrigerating

Makes 8 servings

4   ounces **PHILADELPHIA Cream Cheese,**
     softened
1   **tablespoon milk *or* half-and-half**
1   **tablespoon sugar**
1½   **cups thawed COOL WHIP Whipped**
     Topping
1   **prepared graham cracker crumb crust**
     (6 ounce *or* 9 inch)
1   **cup cold milk *or* half-and-half**
1   **can (16 ounces) pumpkin**
2   **packages (4-serving size *each)* JELL-O**
     Vanilla Flavor Instant Pudding & Pie
     Filling
1   **teaspoon ground cinnamon**
½   **teaspoon ground ginger**
¼   **teaspoon ground cloves**

Mix cream cheese, 1 tablespoon milk and sugar in large bowl with wire whisk until smooth. Gently stir in whipped topping. Spread on bottom of crust.

Pour 1 cup cold milk into large bowl. Add pumpkin, pudding mixes and spices. Beat with wire whisk 2 minutes. (Mixture will be thick.) Spread over cream cheese layer.

Refrigerate 4 hours or until set. Garnish with additional whipped topping and chocolate-dipped pecan halves. Store leftover pie in refrigerator.

Cranberry *Walnut* Pudding Pie

Prep time: 20 minutes plus refrigerating

Makes 10 servings

1½ cups cold milk
2   packages (4-serving size *each*) JELL-O
    Vanilla Flavor Instant Pudding & Pie
    Filling
1   tub (8 ounces) COOL WHIP Whipped
    Topping, thawed
1   prepared graham cracker crumb crust
    (6 ounce or 9 inch)
1   can (16 ounces) whole berry cranberry
    sauce, divided
½   cup toasted chopped walnuts

Pour cold milk into large bowl. Add pudding mixes. Beat with wire whisk 1 minute. (Mixture will be thick.) Gently stir in ½ of the whipped topping.

Spread ½ of the pudding mixture on bottom of crust. Spread ½ of the cranberry sauce over pudding mixture in crust. Sprinkle with walnuts. Spread remaining pudding mixture over walnuts.

Refrigerate 4 hours or until set. Garnish with remaining whipped topping, fresh cranberries and lime peel. Serve with remaining cranberry sauce. Store leftover pie in refrigerator.

Bran Cereal Muffins
(recipe, page 122)

Cranberry Orange Nut
Bread (recipe, page 126)

BAKING
HOLIDAY
MEMORIES

Gathered around the stove is
where many of the season's best moments
take place. Round up your baking helpers,
then choose from this sampling of
irresistible quick breads, scones, muffins,
brownies and snack cakes. The recipes
are simple and a perfect way to get your
whole family in the spirit of the holiday.

Bran Cereal Muffins

(Photo on pages 120–121.)

Prep time: 15 minutes   Baking time: 25 minutes

Makes 12

1	**cup flour**
1	**tablespoon CALUMET Baking Powder**
½	**teaspoon ground cinnamon**
½	**teaspoon salt**
2½	**cups POST Raisin Bran Cereal**
1	**cup milk**
1	**egg**
⅓	**cup firmly packed brown sugar**
⅓	**cup oil**

Mix flour, baking powder, cinnamon and salt in large bowl. Mix cereal and milk in another bowl; let stand 5 minutes. Stir in egg, brown sugar and oil. Add to flour mixture; stir just until moistened. (Batter will be lumpy.)

Spoon batter into greased or paper-lined muffin pan, filling each cup ⅔ full.

Bake at 400°F for 25 minutes or until golden brown. Serve warm.

Crumble Top Banana *Muffins*

Prep time: 15 minutes   Baking time: 20 minutes

Makes 12

Muffins

1¼	**cups flour**
1	**tablespoon CALUMET Baking Powder**
⅛	**teaspoon salt**
1	**egg *or* 2 egg whites**
½	**cup skim milk**
⅓	**cup firmly packed brown sugar**
3	**tablespoons oil**
1½	**cups POST SELECTS BANANA NUT CRUNCH Cereal**
1	**cup finely chopped bananas**

Crumble Topping

½	**cup POST SELECTS BANANA NUT CRUNCH Cereal, slightly crushed**
1	**tablespoon brown sugar**
½	**teaspoon ground cinnamon**
1	**teaspoon oil**

Muffins: Mix flour, baking powder and salt in large bowl. Beat egg in small bowl; stir in milk, brown sugar and oil. Add to flour mixture; stir just until moistened. (Batter will be lumpy.) Stir in cereal and bananas.

Spoon batter into greased or paper-lined muffin pan, filling each cup ⅔ full.

Crumble Topping: Mix slightly crushed cereal, brown sugar and cinnamon. Drizzle with oil; stir until crumbly. Sprinkle evenly over muffins.

Bake in preheated 400°F oven for 20 minutes or until lightly browned. Serve warm.

Bacon Morning *Muffins*

Prep time: 10 minutes   Baking time: 15 minutes

Makes 12

12 slices **LOUIS RICH Turkey Bacon,*** cut into
¼-inch pieces

1¼ cups flour

1 cup quick-cooking oats

2 teaspoons **CALUMET Baking Powder**

½ cup skim milk

⅓ cup honey

¼ cup corn oil

2 large egg whites

Mix turkey bacon, flour, oats and baking powder in large bowl. Add remaining ingredients; stir just until moistened. (Batter will be lumpy.)

Spoon batter into muffin pan sprayed with no stick cooking spray or into paper-lined muffin pan, filling each cup ⅔ full.

Bake at 400°F for 15 minutes. Serve with PHILADELPHIA FREE Soft Fat Free Cream Cheese with Garden Vegetables, if desired. Refrigerate or freeze leftover muffins.

***Note:** Do not substitute regular pork bacon for turkey bacon in this recipe.

Easy Cereal Coffee Cake

Prep time: 10 minutes   Baking time: 30 minutes

Makes 8 servings

2 **cups buttermilk baking mix**
½ **cup firmly packed brown sugar, divided**
2 **cups POST HONEY BUNCHES OF OATS Cereal, any variety, divided**
1 **egg**
1 **cup milk**
½ **teaspoon ground cinnamon**
2 **tablespoons butter *or* margarine**

Mix baking mix, ¼ cup of the brown sugar and 1 cup of the cereal in large bowl.

Beat egg in small bowl; stir in milk. Add to dry mixture; stir just until moistened. Pour into greased 8-inch square baking pan.

Mix remaining 1 cup cereal, remaining ¼ cup brown sugar and cinnamon in small bowl. Cut in butter until mixture resembles coarse crumbs. Sprinkle over batter.

Bake at 375°F for 30 minutes or until toothpick inserted in center comes out clean. Serve warm.

Cranberry Orange Nut Bread

(Photo on pages 120–121.)

Prep time: 20 minutes   Baking time: 1 hour and 15 minutes plus cooling

Makes 1 loaf

1¾ **cups flour**
1 **cup sugar**
1 **tablespoon CALUMET Baking Powder**
¼ **teaspoon salt**
2 **cups POST Raisin Bran Cereal**
1 **cup milk**
1 **egg**
⅓ **cup orange juice**
¼ **cup oil**
1 **tablespoon grated orange peel**
1 **cup fresh cranberries, coarsely chopped**
½ **cup chopped pecans**

Mix flour, sugar, baking powder and salt in large bowl. Mix cereal and milk in another bowl; let stand 5 minutes. Stir in egg, juice, oil and peel. Add to flour mixture; stir just until moistened. (Batter will be lumpy.) Stir in cranberries and pecans.

Pour into greased 9×5-inch loaf pan.

Bake at 350°F for 1 hour and 15 minutes or until toothpick inserted in center comes out clean. Cool 10 minutes. Remove from pan. Cool completely on wire rack.

Note: For easier slicing, wrap bread and store overnight.

Coffee Pumpkin Bread with *Coffee Frosting*

Prep time: 10 minutes   Baking time: 45 minutes plus cooling

Makes 12 servings

1	package (14 ounces) pumpkin bread mix
1¼	cups brewed double strength MAXWELL HOUSE Coffee, any variety, cooled, divided
4	squares BAKER'S Semi-Sweet Baking Chocolate, coarsely chopped (optional)
2	tablespoons butter *or* margarine, melted
3	cups powdered sugar

Prepare bread mix as directed on package, substituting 1 cup of the coffee for water. Gently stir in chopped chocolate. Bake and cool as directed.

Stir remaining ¼ cup coffee into butter in small bowl. Gradually beat coffee mixture into sugar in large bowl with electric mixer on low speed until well blended and smooth.

Frost bread with frosting.

Mini Coffee Pumpkin Loaves:

Prepare as directed, dividing batter evenly into 3 (5¾×3½-inch) disposable mini loaf pans. Bake at 350°F for 40 minutes or until done. Cool and frost as directed.

Sticky Bun Ring

Prep time: 15 minutes   Baking time: 45 minutes plus cooling

Makes 12 servings

4 **cups POST SELECTS BANANA NUT CRUNCH Cereal**
1⅓ **cups firmly packed brown sugar, divided**
⅔ **cup butter *or* margarine, melted**
4 **cans (7½ ounces *each*) refrigerated buttermilk biscuits**

Lightly crush cereal in zipper-style plastic bag. Add ⅔ cup of the sugar; shake to mix well.

Mix remaining ⅔ cup sugar and butter in small bowl.

Cut each biscuit into quarters. Dip, a few at a time, in butter mixture. Add to cereal mixture; shake to coat well. Place in greased 12-cup fluted tube pan or 10-inch tube pan. Sprinkle with any remaining cereal mixture. Drizzle with any remaining butter mixture.

Bake at 350°F for 45 minutes or until golden brown. Cool in pan 10 minutes; invert onto serving dish. Serve warm. Garnish with fresh cranberries and apple slices.

Bacon, Cheddar and *Chive Scones*

Prep time: 15 minutes   Baking time: 16 minutes

Makes 16

2   cups flour
2   teaspoons CALUMET Baking Powder
¼   cup (½ stick) butter *or* margarine
3   eggs, divided
½   cup light cream *or* half-and-half
1½ cups KRAFT Natural Shredded Sharp
     Cheddar Cheese
8   slices OSCAR MAYER Center Cut Bacon,
     crisply cooked, crumbled
1   tablespoon chopped fresh chives
1   tablespoon water

Mix flour and baking powder in large bowl. Cut in butter using pastry blender or knives until coarse crumbs form. Beat 2 of the eggs and cream in medium bowl. Add to flour mixture; stir just until moistened.

Stir in cheese, bacon and chives. Shape into ball. Knead dough 10 times on lightly floured surface. Roll out to 12×6-inch rectangle.

Cut into 8 (3-inch) squares; cut each square in half diagonally. Place on lightly greased cookie sheet. Mix remaining egg and water in small bowl. Brush top of scones with egg mixture.

Bake at 425°F for 14 to 16 minutes or until lightly browned. Serve warm.

Easy Carrot Cake

Prep time: 25 minutes   Baking time: 35 minutes plus cooling

Makes 10 to 12 servings

1¼ cups **MIRACLE WHIP Salad Dressing**
1 **package (2-layer size) yellow cake mix**
4 **eggs**
¼ **cup water**
2 **teaspoons ground cinnamon**
2 **cups finely shredded carrots**
½ **cup chopped walnuts**
1 **package (8 ounces) PHILADELPHIA Cream Cheese, softened**
1 **tablespoon vanilla**
3 **to 3½ cups sifted powdered sugar**

Beat salad dressing, cake mix, eggs, water and cinnamon with electric mixer on medium speed until well blended. Stir in carrots and walnuts. Pour into greased 13×9-inch baking pan.

Bake at 350°F for 30 to 35 minutes or until toothpick inserted in center comes out clean. Cool completely.

Beat cream cheese and vanilla with electric mixer on medium speed until well blended. Gradually add sugar, beating well after each addition. Frost cake.

Cake Mix Magic

There's a secret KRAFT ingredient in Easy Carrot Cake (recipe above). Adding MIRACLE WHIP Salad Dressing to the cake mix gives the finished cake a delicate moistness and an unbeatable rich flavor. Skeptical? Try one bite, and you'll become a believer.

Holiday *Coconut* Cake

Prep time: 20 minutes plus refrigerating   Baking time: 30 minutes plus cooling

Makes 15 to 18 servings

1   **package (2-layer size) yellow cake mix *or* yellow cake mix with pudding in the mix**
1½   **cups milk**
½   **cup sugar**
2   **cups BAKER'S ANGEL FLAKE Coconut, divided**
1   **tub (8 ounces) COOL WHIP Whipped Topping, thawed**

Prepare and bake cake in 13×9-inch baking pan as directed on package. Cool in pan 15 minutes. Pierce cake with large fork at ½-inch intervals.

Mix milk, sugar and ½ cup of the coconut in medium saucepan. Bring to boil. Reduce heat to low; simmer 1 minute. Spoon over warm cake, spreading coconut evenly over top. Cool completely.

Stir ½ cup of the coconut into whipped topping. Spread over cake. Sprinkle with remaining 1 cup coconut.

Refrigerate 6 hours or overnight. Garnish with pineapple chunks, orange slices, orange peel and fresh mint leaves. Store leftover cake in refrigerator.

Cinnamon-Nut Sour Cream Cake

Prep time: 20 minutes   Baking time: 1 hour 25 minutes plus cooling

Makes 16 servings

3	**cups flour**
½	**teaspoon baking soda**
1	**cup (2 sticks) butter *or* margarine**
2½	**cups granulated sugar, divided**
1	**teaspoon vanilla**
6	**eggs**
1	**cup BREAKSTONE'S *or* KNUDSEN Sour Cream**
1	**teaspoon ground cinnamon**
1	**cup chopped walnuts**
	Powdered Sugar Glaze

Mix flour and baking soda in medium bowl. Beat butter and 2¼ cups of the granulated sugar in large bowl with electric mixer on medium speed until light and fluffy. Blend in vanilla. Add eggs, 1 at a time, beating well after each addition. Add flour mixture alternately with sour cream, beating after each addition until smooth.

Pour ½ of the batter into a greased and floured 12-cup fluted tube pan or 10-inch tube pan. Mix remaining ¼ cup granulated sugar and cinnamon; stir in walnuts. Sprinkle over batter. Top with remaining batter.

Bake at 325°F for 1 hour and 15 minutes to 1 hour and 25 minutes or until toothpick inserted in center comes out clean. Cool 10 minutes; remove from pan. Cool completely on wire rack. Drizzle with Powdered Sugar Glaze. Garnish with sliced kumquats and fresh orange leaves.

Powdered Sugar Glaze: Mix 1 cup sifted powdered sugar and 1 tablespoon milk in small bowl. Mix in additional milk, 1 teaspoon at a time, until glaze is smooth and of a drizzling consistency.

One Bowl *Cream Cheese* Brownies

Prep time: 20 minutes   Baking time: 40 minutes plus cooling

Makes 2 dozen

4   squares BAKER'S Unsweetened Baking
    Chocolate
¾   cup (1½ sticks) butter *or* margarine
2   cups sugar
4   eggs
1   teaspoon vanilla
1   cup flour
1   cup coarsely chopped nuts (optional)
1   package (8 ounces) PHILADELPHIA Cream
    Cheese, softened
⅓   cup sugar
1   egg
2   tablespoons flour

Grease 13×9-inch baking pan. Heat oven to 350°F (325°F for glass baking dish).

Microwave chocolate and butter in large microwavable bowl on HIGH 2 minutes or until butter is melted. Stir until chocolate is completely melted.

Stir 2 cups sugar into chocolate until well blended. Mix in 4 eggs and vanilla. Stir in 1 cup flour and nuts until well blended. Spread batter in pan.

Beat cream cheese, ⅓ cup sugar, 1 egg and 2 tablespoons flour in same bowl until well blended. Spoon mixture over brownie batter. Cut through batter with knife several times to create marble effect.

Bake for 40 minutes or until toothpick inserted in center comes out with fudgy crumbs. DO NOT OVERBAKE. Cool in pan. Cut into squares.

One Bowl GERMAN'S® Sweet *Chocolate* Brownies

Prep time: 10 minutes   Baking time: 40 minutes plus cooling

Makes 16

1 **package (4 ounces) BAKER'S GERMAN'S Sweet Baking Chocolate**
¼ **cup (½ stick) butter *or* margarine**
¾ **cup firmly packed brown sugar, divided**
2 **eggs**
½ **cup flour**
1 **cup chopped pecans, divided**
1⅓ **cups (3½ ounces) BAKER'S ANGEL FLAKE Coconut**
¼ **cup milk**

Line 8-inch square baking pan with foil, extending over edges to form handles. Grease foil. Heat oven to 350°F (325°F for glass baking dish).

Microwave chocolate and butter in large microwavable bowl on HIGH 1½ minutes or until butter is melted. Stir until chocolate is completely melted.

Stir ½ cup of the brown sugar into chocolate until well blended. Mix in eggs. Stir in flour and ½ cup of the pecans until well blended. Spread batter in pan.

Mix coconut, remaining ½ cup pecans and remaining ¼ cup brown sugar in same bowl. Stir in milk until well blended. Spoon mixture evenly over brownie batter.

Bake for 40 minutes or until toothpick inserted in center comes out with fudgy crumbs. DO NOT OVERBAKE. Cool in pan. Run knife around edges of pan to loosen brownies from sides. Lift from pan using foil as handles. Cut into squares.

One Bowl *Brownies*

Prep time: 15 minutes   Baking time: 30 minutes plus cooling

Makes 2 dozen

4   **squares BAKER'S Unsweetened Baking Chocolate**
¾   **cup (1½ sticks) butter *or* margarine**
2   **cups sugar**
3   **eggs**
1   **teaspoon vanilla**
1   **cup flour**
1   **cup coarsely chopped nuts (optional)**

Line 13×9-inch baking pan with foil extending over edges to form handles. Grease foil. Heat oven to 350°F (325°F for glass baking dish).

Microwave chocolate and butter in microwavable bowl on HIGH 2 minutes or until butter is melted. Stir until chocolate is completely melted.

Stir sugar into chocolate until blended. Mix in eggs and vanilla. Stir in flour and nuts. Spread batter in pan.

Bake for 30 minutes or until toothpick inserted in center comes out with fudgy crumbs. DO NOT OVERBAKE. Cool in pan. Lift from pan using foil as handles. Cut into squares or into decorative shapes with cookie cutters.

Chocolate Peppermint Trees:

Prepare, bake and cool as directed. Cut cooled brownies into 21 triangles (see diagram below for cutting instructions). Drizzle with 4 squares melted BAKER'S Premium White Baking Chocolate. Insert straight pieces of miniature candy canes in bottoms of triangles to form trunks. Crush candy cane tops; sprinkle over trees. Makes 21.

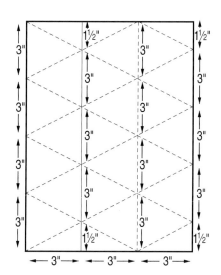

Chocolate Peppermint
Trees (recipe opposite
page)

PHIADELPHIA® Cream Cheese ookies—counterclockwise from op left: Preserve Thumbprints, Chocolate Mint Cutouts, nowmen, Choco-Orange Slices (recipes, pages 142 and 143)

COOKIE AND GIFT CLASSICS

Touch the hearts of loved ones near and far away by giving them gifts from your kitchen. Festive cookies, rich candies or flavorful loaves of quick bread will convey your holiday thoughts in a delicious fashion. And, to tell the recipients that they're extra-special, package each gift in a decorative container or colorful gift wrap.

PHILADELPHIA® Cream Cheese *Cookies*

(Photo on pages 140–141.)

Prep time: 20 minutes plus refrigerating
Baking time: 12 to 20 minutes per cookie sheet, depending on variation, plus cooling

Makes 3 cups dough

1   **package (8 ounces) PHILADELPHIA Cream Cheese, softened**
¾   **cup butter**
1   **cup powdered sugar**
2¼   **cups flour**
½   **teaspoon baking soda**

Beat cream cheese, butter and sugar with electric mixer on medium speed until well blended.

Add flour and baking soda; mix well. Use dough in 2 of the following variations. Makes 3 cups dough.

Chocolate Mint Cutouts: Add

¼ teaspoon mint extract and a few drops green food coloring to 1½ cups cookie dough; mix well. Refrigerate 30 minutes.

Roll dough to ⅛-inch thickness on lightly floured surface; cut with assorted 3-inch cookie cutters. Place on ungreased cookie sheets. Bake at 325°F for 10 to 12 minutes or until edges begin to brown. Remove from cookie sheets. Cool on wire rack. Store in airtight container.

Melt ¼ cup BAKER'S Semi-Sweet Real Chocolate Chips on low heat, stirring until smooth. Drizzle over cookies.

Makes about 3 dozen.

Snowmen: Add ¼ teaspoon vanilla to 1½ cups cookie dough; mix well. Refrigerate 30 minutes.

For each snowman, shape dough into 2 small balls, one slightly larger than the other. Place balls, overlapping slightly, on ungreased cookie sheets; flatten with bottom of glass. Bake at 325°F for 18 to 20 minutes or until light golden brown. Remove from cookie sheets. Cool on wire rack. Store in airtight container.

Sprinkle each snowman with sifted powdered sugar. Decorate with icing as desired. Cut miniature peanut butter cups in half for hats.

Makes about 2 dozen.

Choco-Orange Slices: Add

1½ teaspoons grated orange peel to 1½ cups cookie dough; mix well. Shape into 8×1½-inch log. Refrigerate 30 minutes.

Cut log into ¼-inch slices. Place on ungreased cookie sheets. Bake at 325°F for 15 to 18 minutes or until edges begin to brown. Remove from cookie sheets. Cool on wire rack. Store in airtight container.

Melt ⅓ cup BAKER'S Semi-Sweet Real Chocolate Chips with 1 tablespoon orange juice and 1 tablespoon orange-flavored liqueur on low heat, stirring until smooth. Dip ½ of each cookie into chocolate mixture; let excess drip off.

Makes about 2½ dozen.

Preserve Thumbprints: Add ½ cup chopped pecans and ½ teaspoon vanilla to 1½ cups cookie dough; mix well. Refrigerate 30 minutes.

Shape dough into 1-inch balls. Place on ungreased cookie sheets. Make an indentation in center of each ball. Fill each indentation with 1 teaspoon preserves. Bake at 325°F for 14 to 16 minutes or until light golden brown. Remove from cookie sheets. Cool on wire rack. Store in airtight container.

Makes about 3½ dozen.

Coconut Shortbread

Prep time: 10 minutes   Baking time: 25 minutes

Makes 36

- ¾ **cup (1½ sticks) butter *or* margarine, softened**
- ½ **cup sugar**
- 1 **teaspoon vanilla**
- 1½ **cups flour**
- 1 **package (7 ounces) BAKER'S ANGEL FLAKE Coconut, lightly toasted (2⅔ cups)**

Line 13×9-inch baking pan with foil extending over edges to form handles. Grease foil.

Beat butter, sugar and vanilla in medium bowl with electric mixer on medium speed 2 minutes or until well blended. Gradually beat in flour on low speed until blended. Stir in coconut. Press dough evenly into prepared pan with hands. Pierce dough with fork at 1-inch intervals all the way through to bottom of pan.

Bake at 325°F for 20 to 25 minutes or until lightly browned. Cool in pan 5 minutes. Run knife around edges of pan to loosen shortbread from sides. Lift from pan using foil as handles. Using star-shaped cookie cutter or large sharp knife, cut warm shortbread into stars or bars. Cool completely. Store in airtight container. Decorate with melted BAKER'S Semi-Sweet Baking Chocolate Squares, if desired.

Sugar *Cookies*

Prep time: 10 minutes plus refrigerating Baking time: 12 minutes per cookie sheet plus cooling

Makes about 4 dozen

2½ **cups flour**
2 **teaspoons CALUMET Baking Powder**
½ **teaspoon salt**
½ **cup (1 stick) butter *or* margarine, softened**
1 **envelope (2-quart pouch) KOOL-AID Sugar-Sweetened Soft Drink Mix, any flavor**
¼ **cup sugar**
2 **eggs**

Mix flour, baking powder and salt in small bowl. Beat butter, soft drink mix and sugar in large bowl with electric mixer on medium speed until light and fluffy. Beat in eggs. Gradually add flour mixture, beating well after each addition.

Divide dough into 2 equal portions; wrap each in plastic wrap. Refrigerate 3 hours or until firm.

Roll out dough, ½ at a time, to ¼-inch thickness on lightly floured surface. Cut into desired shapes with lightly floured cookie cutters. Place on ungreased cookie sheets, 2 inches apart.

Bake at 375°F for 10 to 12 minutes or until edges are lightly browned. Remove from cookie sheets. Cool on wire racks. Store in airtight container. Decorate with ready-to-spread frosting, if desired.

Snowflake Macaroons

Prep time: 15 minutes   Baking time: 20 minutes per cookie sheet plus cooling

Makes 3 dozen

1   package (7 ounces) BAKER'S
      ANGEL FLAKE Coconut (2⅔ cups)
⅔   cup sugar
6   tablespoons flour
¼   teaspoon salt
4   egg whites
1   teaspoon almond extract

Mix coconut, sugar, flour and salt in bowl. Stir in egg whites and extract until blended. Drop by teaspoonfuls onto lightly greased and floured cookie sheets.

Bake at 325°F for 20 minutes or until edges are golden brown. Immediately remove from cookie sheets. Cool on wire racks. Store in airtight container.

Chocolate Macaroons: Stir in 2 squares melted BAKER'S Semi-Sweet Baking Chocolate with egg whites.

Have Cookies Will Travel

When sending cookies through the mail, prevent ending up with a box of crumbs by choosing bar cookies or other soft types. Avoid those that have frosting or pointed edges. Wrap different kinds of cookies separately. Good containers include cookie tins, rigid boxes and coffee or shortening cans. Pack the containers in a sturdy outer box with plenty of room for cushion. Pad the boxes with foam pellets or plastic bubble wrap.

Snowflake Macaroons
and Chocolate
Macaroons (recipes
opposite page)

Breakfast Biscotti

Prep time: 30 minutes   Baking time: 42 minutes plus cooling

Makes about 2 dozen

2   **cups flour**
1½   **teaspoons CALUMET Baking Powder**
¼   **teaspoon salt**
½   **cup (1 stick) butter *or* margarine**
⅔   **cup sugar**
2   **eggs**
1   **medium fully ripe banana, mashed**
1   **teaspoon vanilla**
1½   **cups POST SELECTS BANANA NUT CRUNCH Cereal**

Mix flour, baking powder and salt in small bowl. Beat butter and sugar in large bowl with electric mixer on medium speed until light and fluffy. Blend in eggs, banana and vanilla. Gradually add flour mixture, beating well after each addition. Stir in cereal.

Divide dough into 2 equal portions. Shape dough into 2 (14×2-inch) logs on greased cookie sheet.

Bake at 325°F for 30 minutes or until lightly browned. Remove from cookie sheet. Place on cutting board; cool 5 minutes. Cut each log, using serrated knife, into diagonal slices about ¾ inch thick. Place slices upright on cookie sheet, ½ inch apart.

Bake 12 minutes or until slightly dry. Remove from cookie sheet. Cool on wire rack. Store in airtight container. Drizzle with melted BAKER'S Semi-Sweet Baking Chocolate Squares or sprinkle with powdered sugar, if desired.

Raisin Thumbprint *Cookies*

(Photo on page 152 and front cover.)

Prep time: 30 minutes   Baking time: 15 minutes per cookie sheet plus cooling

Makes about 3½ dozen

1	cup (2 sticks) butter *or* margarine
¾	cup powdered sugar
¼	teaspoon salt
1¼	teaspoons vanilla
1¾	cups flour
1½	cups POST Raisin Bran Cereal
	Jam *or* preserves

Beat butter in large bowl with electric mixer on medium speed to soften. Gradually add powdered sugar and salt, beating well after each addition. Add vanilla. Stir in flour and cereal.

Shape dough into 1-inch balls. Place on ungreased cookie sheets. Make an indentation in center of each ball.

Bake at 375°F for 12 to 15 minutes or until lightly browned. Remove from cookie sheets. Cool on wire racks. Store in airtight container. Fill indentations with jam. Sprinkle with additional powdered sugar, if desired.

Crispy Oatmeal *Raisin* Cookies

Prep time: 15 minutes   Baking time: 8 minutes per cookie sheet plus cooling

Makes 5 dozen

1½ **cups flour**
1 **teaspoon baking soda**
1½ **cups (3 sticks) butter *or* margarine,**
    softened
⅔ **cup *each* firmly packed brown sugar**
    and granulated sugar
1 **egg**
1 **teaspoon vanilla**
2 **cups POST GRAPE-NUTS Cereal**
2 **cups quick-cooking oats**
1 **cup raisins**

Mix flour and baking soda in small bowl.
Beat butter in large bowl with electric mixer
on medium speed to soften. Gradually add
sugars, beating until light and fluffy. Beat
in egg and vanilla. Gradually add flour
mixture, beating well after each addition.
Stir in cereal, oats and raisins.

Drop by rounded tablespoonfuls onto
ungreased cookie sheets.

Bake at 375°F for 8 minutes or until
lightly browned. Cool 1 minute; remove
from cookie sheets. Cool on wire racks.
Store in airtight container.

Peanut Butter Drop Cookies

Prep time: 15 minutes   Baking time: 12 minutes per cookie sheet plus cooling

Makes 4 dozen

1¼ **cups flour**
 1 **teaspoon baking soda**
 ¼ **teaspoon salt**
 ½ **cup (1 stick) butter *or* margarine,
      softened**
 1 **cup sugar**
 1 **egg**
 1 **teaspoon vanilla**
 ½ **cup peanut butter**
 2 **tablespoons milk**
1½ **cups POST HONEY BUNCHES OF OATS
      Cereal, any variety**

Mix flour, baking soda and salt in small bowl. Beat butter in large bowl with electric mixer on medium speed to soften. Gradually add sugar, beating until light and fluffy. Beat in egg, vanilla and peanut butter. Gradually add flour mixture alternately with milk, beating well after each addition. Stir in cereal.

Drop by rounded teaspoonfuls onto ungreased cookie sheets.

Bake at 350°F for 10 to 12 minutes or until edges are golden brown. Cool slightly. Remove from cookie sheets. Cool on wire racks. Store in airtight container.

Raisin Thumbprint
Cookies
(recipe, page 149)

Cereal Peanut Butter Bars
(recipe opposite page)

Cereal Peanut Butter Bars

Prep time: 20 minutes

Makes about 3 dozen

1½ **cups chunky peanut butter**
⅔ **cup maple-flavored syrup**
⅔ **cup sugar**
3 **cups POST HONEY BUNCHES OF OATS Cereal, any variety**
4 **squares BAKER'S Semi-Sweet Baking Chocolate, melted**

Line 13×9-inch baking pan with foil extending over edges to form handles. Grease foil.

Microwave peanut butter, syrup and sugar in large microwavable bowl on HIGH 3 minutes, stirring every minute.

Pour syrup mixture over cereal in large bowl; mix to coat well. Press evenly into prepared pan with hands.

Spread melted chocolate evenly over cereal mixture. Let stand or refrigerate until chocolate is firm. Lift from pan using foil as handles. Cut into bars. Garnish with chopped peanuts and candies. Store in refrigerator.

Coffee Chocolate *Chunk Cookies*

Prep time: 10 minutes   Baking time: 12 minutes per cookie sheet plus cooling

Makes 5 dozen

1¾   **cups flour**
¼   **teaspoon baking soda**
¾   **cup (1½ sticks) butter *or* margarine**
¾   **cup granulated sugar**
½   **cup firmly packed brown sugar**
¼   **cup chilled freshly brewed strong MAXWELL HOUSE Coffee**
1   **egg**
1   **teaspoon vanilla**
1   **package (8 squares) BAKER'S Semi-Sweet Baking Chocolate, cut into chunks**
1½   **cups chopped walnuts**

Mix flour and baking soda in small bowl. Beat butter in large bowl with electric mixer on medium speed to soften. Gradually add sugars, beating until light and fluffy. Beat in coffee, egg and vanilla. Gradually add flour mixture, beating well after each addition. Stir in chocolate and walnuts.

Drop dough by rounded teaspoonfuls, 2 inches apart, onto ungreased cookie sheets.

Bake at 375°F for 10 to 12 minutes or until golden brown. Remove from cookie sheets. Cool on wire rack. Store in airtight container.

Kris Kringle Cookies

Prep time: 15 minutes   Baking time: 12 minutes per cookie sheet plus cooling

Makes about 3 dozen

- ½ **cup (1 stick) butter *or* margarine,** softened
- ½ **cup granulated sugar**
- ¼ **cup firmly packed brown sugar**
- 1 **egg**
- ½ **teaspoon vanilla**
- 1 **cup flour**
- 1 **teaspoon baking soda**
- ¼ **teaspoon salt**
- 6 **squares BAKER'S Semi-Sweet Baking Chocolate, chopped**
- 2 **cups toasted chopped walnuts**
- 1½ **cups dried fruit**

Beat butter and sugars in large bowl with electric mixer on medium speed until light and fluffy. Beat in egg and vanilla. Mix in flour, baking soda and salt. Stir in chocolate, walnuts and dried fruit. Drop by rounded tablespoonfuls, 1½ inches apart, onto ungreased cookie sheets.

Bake at 375°F for 12 minutes or until golden brown. Cool 3 minutes; remove from cookie sheets. Cool on wire rack. Store in airtight container.

White & Bright Cookies:

Prepare as directed, substituting BAKER'S Premium White Baking Chocolate, almonds and chopped dried apricots for Semi-Sweet Baking Chocolate, walnuts and dried fruit.

SUGAR BEAR™ Paw
Cookies (recipe,
page 158)

Fruity PEBBLES®
Wreaths (recipe
opposite page)

Fruity PEBBLES® Wreaths

Prep time: 10 minutes

Makes 9

2   **tablespoons butter *or* margarine**

2⅔ **cups miniature marshmallows**

4½ **cups POST Fruity PEBBLES Cereal**

Microwave butter in large microwavable bowl on HIGH 30 seconds or until melted. Add marshmallows; toss to coat with butter. Microwave on HIGH 1 minute more or until smooth when stirred, stirring after 30 seconds.

Add cereal immediately; mix lightly until well coated.

Shape ½ cup of the cereal mixture with greased hands into wreath shape. Place on wax paper-lined tray. Repeat with remaining cereal mixture. Cool. Garnish with bows made from chewy fruit snack rolls and assorted candies.

PEBBLES is a registered trademark of Hanna-Barbera Productions, Inc., used with permission.

SUGAR BEAR™ *Paw Cookies*

(Photo on page 156.)

Prep time: 10 minutes   Baking time: 10 minutes per cookie sheet plus cooling

Makes about 5 dozen

1 cup (2 sticks) butter *or* margarine, softened
1½ cups firmly packed brown sugar
2 eggs
1 teaspoon vanilla
2 cups flour
1 teaspoon baking soda
3 cups POST GOLDEN CRISP Sweetened Puffed Wheat Cereal
1 package (8 squares) BAKER'S Semi-Sweet Baking Chocolate
POST GOLDEN CRISP Sweetened Puffed Wheat Cereal

Beat butter, sugar, eggs and vanilla in large bowl with electric mixer on medium speed until light and fluffy. Mix in flour and baking soda. Stir in 3 cups cereal. Drop dough by heaping teaspoonfuls, 2 inches apart, onto ungreased cookie sheets.

Bake at 350°F for 8 to 10 minutes or until golden brown. Remove from cookie sheets. Cool on wire rack.

Melt chocolate as directed on package. Dip ½ of each cookie into melted chocolate; let excess drip off. Immediately sprinkle with additional cereal for paws. Place on wax paper-lined tray. Refrigerate until chocolate is firm. Store in refrigerator.

Chocolate Pizza

Prep time: 15 minutes plus refrigerating   Microwave time: 6 minutes or Stovetop cooking time: 10 minutes

Makes 10 to 12 servings

1 **package (12 ounces) BAKER'S Semi-Sweet Real Chocolate Chips**
1 **pound white almond bark, divided**
2 **cups miniature marshmallows**
1 **cup crisp rice cereal**
1 **cup peanuts**
1 **jar (6 ounces) red maraschino cherries, drained, cut in half**
3 **tablespoons green maraschino cherries, drained, quartered**
⅓ **cup BAKER'S ANGEL FLAKE Coconut**
1 **teaspoon oil**

Microwave chips and 14 ounces of the almond bark in 2-quart microwavable bowl on HIGH 2 minutes; stir. Continue microwaving 1 to 2 minutes or until smooth when stirred, stirring every 30 seconds.

Stir in marshmallows, cereal and peanuts. Pour onto greased 12-inch pizza pan. Top with cherries; sprinkle with coconut.

Microwave remaining 2 ounces almond bark and oil in 1-cup glass measuring cup 1 minute; stir. Continue microwaving 30 seconds to 1 minute or until smooth when stirred, stirring every 15 seconds. Drizzle over coconut.

Refrigerate until firm. Store at room temperature.

To cook on stove:

Melt chips and 14 ounces of the almond bark in large saucepan on low heat, stirring until smooth. Remove from heat.

Stir in marshmallows, cereal and peanuts. Pour onto greased 12-inch pizza pan. Top with cherries; sprinkle with coconut.

Melt remaining 2 ounces almond bark with oil on low heat, stirring until smooth. Drizzle over coconut.

Refrigerate until firm. Store at room temperature.

Individual Chocolate Pizzas:

Prepare as directed except spoon chocolate mixture onto greased cookie sheet, forming 3 (7-inch) or 4 (6-inch) circles with back of wooden spoon. Continue as directed.

Cranberry *Crunchers*

Prep time: 10 minutes   Baking time: 15 minutes

Makes about 3½ dozen

1 **box (13 ounces) POST SELECTS CRANBERRY ALMOND CRUNCH Cereal (6 cups)**
1 **can (14 ounces) sweetened condensed milk**
½ **teaspoon almond extract**

Mix cereal, condensed milk and almond extract in large bowl until well blended.

Press firmly into greased foil-lined 13×9-inch baking pan with lightly greased hands.

Bake at 325°F for 15 minutes or until golden brown. Immediately lift bars from pan using foil. Cool on wire rack 10 minutes; remove foil. Cool completely on wire rack. Cut into bars.

Variation: Prepare as directed, substituting POST SELECTS GREAT GRAINS Whole Grain Cereal *or* BANANA NUT CRUNCH Cereal for CRANBERRY ALMOND CRUNCH Cereal.

Fantasy *Fudge*

Prep time: 10 minutes plus cooling   Cooking time: 15 minutes

Makes about 3 pounds

¾ **cup (1½ sticks) butter *or* margarine**
3 **cups sugar**
1 **can (5 ounces) evaporated milk***
   (⅔ cup)
1 **package (12 ounces) BAKER'S**
   Semi-Sweet Real Chocolate Chips
1 **jar (7 ounces) marshmallow creme**
1 **cup chopped nuts (optional)**
1 **teaspoon vanilla**

Lightly grease 13×9-inch or 9-inch square pan.

Mix butter, sugar and milk in heavy 2½- to 3-quart saucepan; bring to full rolling boil on medium heat, stirring constantly.

Continue boiling 5 minutes on medium heat or until candy thermometer reaches 234°F, stirring constantly to prevent scorching. Remove from heat.

Gradually stir in chips until melted. Add remaining ingredients; mix well.

Pour into prepared pan. Cool at room temperature; cut into squares.

*Note: Do not substitute sweetened condensed milk for evaporated milk.

Holiday *Peppermint* Candies

Prep time: 30 minutes plus refrigerating

Makes 5 dozen

4   ounces PHILADELPHIA Cream Cheese, softened
1   tablespoon butter *or* margarine
1   tablespoon light corn syrup
¼   teaspoon peppermint extract *or* a few drops peppermint oil
4   cups powdered sugar
    Green and red food coloring
    Sifted powdered sugar
    Green, red and white decorating icing (optional)

Beat cream cheese, butter, corn syrup and extract in large bowl with electric mixer on medium speed until well blended. Gradually add 4 cups sugar; mix well.

Divide mixture into thirds. Knead a few drops green food coloring into first third; repeat with red food coloring and second third. Wrap each third in plastic wrap.

Working with 1 color mixture at a time, shape into ¾-inch balls. Place on wax paper-lined cookie sheet. Flatten each ball with bottom of glass that has been lightly dipped in sifted powdered sugar.

Repeat with remaining mixtures. Decorate with icing. Store candies in refrigerator.

Cereal *Peanut Butter* Cups

Prep time: 20 minutes plus refrigerating

Makes 12

⅓   **cup peanut butter**
¼   **cup (½ stick) butter *or* margarine**
3   **cups miniature marshmallows**
3   **cups POST Cocoa PEBBLES Cereal**
¾   **cup powdered sugar**
1   **tablespoon milk**

Melt peanut butter and butter in medium saucepan on low heat. Add marshmallows; stir until melted. Remove from heat.

Add cereal; mix to coat well. Spoon ¼ cup of the mixture into each of 12 paper-lined muffin cups. Refrigerate about 1 hour or until firm.

Mix sugar and milk. Drizzle over cereal mixture. Store in refrigerator.

PEBBLES is a registered trademark of Hanna-Barbera Productions, Inc., used with permission.

Chewy Caramel Bars

Prep time: 20 minutes plus refrigerating

Makes 32

8   **cups POST GOLDEN CRISP Sweetened Puffed Wheat Cereal**
1   **cup peanuts**
1   **package (14 ounces) caramels, unwrapped**
2   **tablespoons water**

Mix cereal and peanuts in large bowl.

Microwave caramels and water in microwavable bowl on HIGH 2 minutes or until caramels are melted, stirring every minute. Pour immediately over cereal mixture. Mix lightly until well coated.

With lightly greased hands, press firmly into greased 13×9-inch pan. Refrigerate until firm. Cut into bars. Store in airtight container.

Chewy Caramel Bars
(recipe opposite
page)

Cereal Peanut
Butter Cups
(recipe opposite
page)

Fudge Balls

Prep time: 10 minutes plus refrigerating

Makes about 2 dozen

1   **package (8 squares) BAKER'S Semi-Sweet Baking Chocolate**
⅓   **cup sweetened condensed milk**
¼   **cup freshly brewed MAXWELL HOUSE *or* YUBAN Coffee**
½   **cup chopped nuts**
1   **teaspoon vanilla**
    Suggested Coatings: MAXWELL HOUSE *or* YUBAN Ground Coffee, unsweetened cocoa, ground nuts, graham cracker crumbs, cookie crumbs, powdered sugar, toasted BAKER'S ANGEL FLAKE Coconut

Microwave chocolate, milk and coffee in large microwavable bowl on HIGH 2 minutes or until chocolate is almost melted, stirring halfway through heating time. Stir until chocolate is completely melted.

Stir in chopped nuts and vanilla. Spread in foil-lined 8-inch square pan.

Refrigerate 2 hours or until firm enough to handle. Shape into 1-inch balls. Roll in desired coatings. Store in refrigerator.

Crunchy *Cocoa* Treats

Prep time: 10 minutes plus refrigerating

Makes 3 dozen

4 cups POST Cocoa PEBBLES Cereal
6 squares BAKER'S Semi-Sweet Baking
    Chocolate
½ cup light corn syrup
1 tablespoon butter *or* margarine
½ teaspoon vanilla

Place cereal in large bowl.

Microwave chocolate, corn syrup and butter in large microwavable bowl on HIGH 2½ minutes, stirring halfway through heating time. Stir until chocolate is completely melted. Stir in vanilla.

Pour chocolate mixture over cereal; mix lightly. With hands slightly moistened with cold water, shape into 1-inch balls. Place on wax paper-lined tray. Refrigerate until firm. Wrap in decorative foil. Store in refrigerator.

PEBBLES is a registered trademark of Hanna-Barbera Productions, Inc., used with permission.

Festive Fruit Bark
and Chocolate
Peanut Butter Marble Bark
(recipes opposite page)

Marble Bark

Prep time: 10 minutes plus refrigerating   Microwave time: 4 minutes

Makes about 1 pound

6 squares BAKER'S Semi-Sweet Baking Chocolate
1 package (6 squares) BAKER'S Premium White Baking Chocolate
1 cup toasted chopped nuts *or* toasted BAKER'S ANGEL FLAKE Coconut, divided

Microwave semi-sweet and white chocolates in separate microwavable bowls on HIGH 2 minutes or until chocolates are almost melted, stirring halfway through heating time. Stir until chocolates are completely melted.

Stir ½ cup of the nuts into each bowl. Alternately spoon melted chocolates onto wax paper-lined cookie sheet or tray. Swirl chocolates together with knife to marbleize.

Refrigerate 1 hour or until firm. Break into pieces.

Festive Fruit Bark: Prepare Marble Bark as directed, omitting Semi-Sweet Baking Chocolate and nuts. Use 2 packages (6 squares *each*) BAKER'S Premium White Baking Chocolate. Stir in ½ cup toasted chopped almonds or pistachios and ½ cup dried cranberries.

Chocolate Peanut Butter Marble Bark: Prepare Marble Bark as directed, omitting nuts and stirring ¼ cup creamy peanut butter into melted white chocolate.

Easy Chocolate *Truffles*

Prep time: 15 minutes plus refrigerating

Makes about 5 dozen candies

1   **package (8 ounces) PHILADELPHIA Cream Cheese, softened**
3   **cups powdered sugar**
1½ **packages (12 squares) BAKER'S Semi-Sweet Baking Chocolate, melted**
1½ **teaspoons vanilla**
    Ground walnuts, unsweetened cocoa *and/or* BAKER'S ANGEL FLAKE Coconut

Beat cream cheese in large bowl with wire whisk or electric mixer until smooth. Gradually add sugar, beating until well blended.

Add melted chocolate and vanilla; mix well. Refrigerate about 1 hour or until firm.

Shape into 1-inch balls. Roll in walnuts, cocoa or coconut. Store in refrigerator.

Easy Spirited Chocolate Truffles:

Prepare as directed except omit vanilla. Divide truffle mixture into thirds. Add 1 tablespoon liqueur (almond, coffee or orange-flavored) to each third of mixture; mix well.

Gift-Giving Cereal Bread

Prep time: 20 minutes   Baking time: 65 minutes plus cooling

Makes 1 loaf

1¾   **cups flour**
⅔   **cup firmly packed light brown sugar**
2   **tablespoons MAXWELL HOUSE Instant Coffee**
2½   **teaspoons CALUMET Baking Powder**
1   **teaspoon salt**
2   **cups POST Raisin Bran**
1⅓   **cups milk**
1   **egg, beaten**
3   **tablespoons butter *or* margarine, melted**

Mix flour, sugar, coffee, baking powder and salt in large bowl. Mix cereal and milk in another bowl. Stir in egg and butter. Add to flour mixture; stir just until moistened. Pour into greased and floured 8×4-inch loaf pan.

Bake at 350°F for 60 to 65 minutes or until toothpick inserted in center comes out clean. Cool 5 minutes; remove from pan. Cool completely on wire rack.

Note: For easier slicing, wrap and store overnight.

Scrumptious Gifts from the Kitchen

For a presentation as special as the gift, try one of these ideas:

• Wrap pieces of candy in colorful foil wrappers, then place them in a striking box or decorative tin. Buy the wrappers at stores that carry cake-decorating supplies. Wrap cookies individually in colorful plastic wrap, then tie each with ribbon.

• Make a "good morning" gift by packing a loaf of bread in a basket lined with a pretty cloth napkin or dish towel. Complete the gift by adding an assortment of small jars of jams and jellies and a container of Russian Tea Mix (recipe, page 173).

• For a sweet little treat for co-workers or other friends, stack a few cookies or pieces of Marble Bark (recipe, page 167) and tie the bundle with cord or ribbon.

Chocolate Banana Bread

Prep time: 20 minutes   Baking time: 55 minutes plus cooling

Makes 1 loaf

2 squares BAKER'S Unsweetened Baking
   Chocolate
1¼ cups flour
1 teaspoon baking soda
½ teaspoon salt
2 eggs
¾ cup firmly packed brown sugar
¾ cup buttermilk
½ cup oil
1 fully ripe banana, mashed (about
   ½ cup)
2½ cups POST SELECTS BANANA NUT CRUNCH
   Cereal, divided
1 teaspoon oil

Microwave chocolate in microwavable bowl on HIGH 1 to 2 minutes or until chocolate is almost melted, stirring halfway through heating time. Stir until chocolate is completely melted.

Mix flour, baking soda and salt in large bowl. Beat eggs in medium bowl; stir in melted chocolate, sugar, buttermilk, ½ cup oil and banana. Add to flour mixture; stir just until moistened. (Batter will be lumpy.) Stir in 2 cups of the cereal. Spoon batter into greased 9×5-inch loaf pan.

Crush remaining ½ cup cereal in small bowl. Drizzle with 1 teaspoon oil. Stir until crumbly. Sprinkle evenly over batter.

Bake at 350°F for 50 to 55 minutes or until toothpick inserted in center comes out clean. Cool 10 minutes; remove from pan. Cool completely on wire rack.

Russian *Tea Mix*

Prep time: 10 minutes

Makes 2 cups mix

1⅓ cups **TANG Brand Orange Flavor Drink Mix**
½ cup **sugar**
⅓ cup **instant tea**
1 teaspoon **ground cinnamon**
½ teaspoon **ground cloves**

Mix all ingredients. Store in tightly covered jar.

For 1 serving, place 1 tablespoon mix into cup. Add ¾ cup boiling water. Stir until mix is dissolved.

For 4 servings (1 quart), place ⅓ cup mix into heatproof pitcher or bowl. Add 4 cups (1 quart) boiling water. Stir until mix is dissolved. Serve with lemon wedges, if desired.

Variations:

For 1 serving of Iced Russian Tea, dissolve 2 tablespoons tea mix in ¾ cup boiling water. Pour over ice cubes in tall glass.

For a reduced-sugar version, reduce sugar to ¼ cup. Substitute 1 cup TANG Brand Orange Flavor Sugar Free Drink Mix for regular drink mix.

Quick Holiday Chicken
Stir-Fry (recipe, page 176)

ON-THE-RUN DINNERS

Everybody's on the run with hockey practice, choir rehearsal, year-end deadlines and holiday get-togethers. In the midst of all these activities, family meals can get short-changed. Now, you can have the dinner situation mastered, even on your busiest days. With these timely suggestions for quick and easy meals, you're home free.

Quick Holiday Chicken Stir-Fry

(Photo on pages 174–175.)

Prep time: 10 minutes   Cooking time: 7 minutes

Makes 4 servings

½ cup **MIRACLE WHIP** *or* **MIRACLE WHIP LIGHT Dressing, divided**

4 **boneless skinless chicken breast halves (about 1¼ pounds), cut into thin strips**

¼ to ½ **teaspoon garlic powder**

3 **cups assorted fresh cut-up vegetables** *or* **1 package (16 ounces) frozen mixed vegetables**

2 **tablespoons soy sauce**

2 **cups hot cooked MINUTE White Rice**

Heat 2 tablespoons of the dressing in skillet on medium-high heat. Add chicken and garlic powder; stir-fry 3 minutes.

Add vegetables; stir-fry 3 minutes or until chicken is cooked through. Reduce heat to medium.

Stir in remaining dressing and soy sauce; simmer 1 minute. Serve over rice.

Just Family Night at Home

During the busy holiday season, circle several at-home nights on the calendar; then settle in with the most important people in your life—your family. Take turns choosing the activity, such as making cookies or other snacks, playing games or planning next year's vacation.

STOVE TOP® One-Dish *Chicken Bake*

Prep time: 10 minutes   Baking time: 35 minutes

Makes 4 servings

1   **package (6 ounces) STOVE TOP Stuffing Mix for Chicken**
1½ **cups hot water**
¼   **cup (½ stick) butter *or* margarine, cut up**
4   **boneless skinless chicken breast halves (about 1¼ pounds)**
1   **can (10¾ ounces) condensed cream of mushroom soup**
⅓   **cup BREAKSTONE'S *or* KNUDSEN Sour Cream *or* milk**

Mix contents of Vegetable/Seasoning Packet, hot water and butter in large bowl until butter is melted. Stir in Stuffing Crumbs just to moisten. Let stand 5 minutes.

Place chicken down center of 12×8-inch baking dish. Mix soup and sour cream; pour over chicken. Spoon some of the stuffing over chicken. Spoon remaining stuffing around chicken.

Bake at 375°F for 35 minutes or until chicken is cooked through. Garnish with red pepper strips and fresh thyme.

Parmesan Chicken Breasts

Prep time: 10 minutes   Baking time: 20 minutes

Makes 6 servings

½ **cup (2 ounces) KRAFT 100% Grated Parmesan Cheese**
¼ **cup seasoned dry bread crumbs**
¼ **teaspoon** *each* **paprika, salt and pepper**
6 **boneless skinless chicken breast halves (about 2 pounds)**
3 **tablespoons butter** *or* **margarine, melted**

Mix cheese, crumbs and seasonings.

Dip chicken in butter; coat with cheese mixture. Place in greased 15×10×1-inch baking pan.

Bake at 400°F for 20 to 25 minutes or until cooked through. Garnish with red and yellow tomato wedges, zucchini curls and fresh basil leaves.

Variation: Prepare as directed, substituting PARM PLUS! Seasoning Blend for KRAFT 100% Grated Parmesan Cheese. Substitute dry bread crumbs for seasoned dry bread crumbs. Omit seasonings.

Garlicky *Chicken* Breasts

Prep time: 5 minutes   Baking time: 25 minutes

Makes 6 servings

1   envelope **GOOD SEASONS Roasted Garlic** *or* **Italian Salad Dressing Mix**

½   **cup (2 ounces) KRAFT 100% Grated Parmesan Cheese**

6   **boneless skinless chicken breast halves (about 2 pounds)**

Mix salad dressing mix and cheese.

Moisten chicken in water; dip in dressing mixture. Place in shallow baking dish.

Bake at 400°F for 20 to 25 minutes or until cooked through. Garnish with fresh basil leaves and carrot and yellow pepper strips.

Turkey Steak & Potatoes

Prep time: 5 minutes   Broiling time: 8 minutes

Makes 4 servings

1   **tablespoon melted butter**
1   **tablespoon olive oil**
1   **tablespoon KRAFT 100% Grated Parmesan Cheese**
½   **teaspoon dry mustard**
¼   **teaspoon garlic powder**
1   **pound LOUIS RICH Breast of Turkey, cut into ½-inch-thick slices**
4   **cups (½ of 28-ounce bag) frozen steak fries**

Mix butter, oil, cheese, mustard and garlic powder.

Place turkey and steak fries in single layer on cookie sheet; brush with ½ of the butter mixture.

Broil on top rack of broiler 4 minutes. Turn turkey and steak fries; brush with remaining butter mixture. Broil 4 minutes or until lightly browned.

SHAKE 'N BAKE® *Pork Chops* and Peaches

Prep time: 10 minutes   Baking time: 20 minutes

Makes 6 to 8 servings

1 **can (15¼ ounces) sliced peaches or pears, undrained**

6 **to 8 pork chops, ½ inch thick**

2 **teaspoons ground ginger (optional)**

1 **packet SHAKE 'N BAKE Seasoned Coating Mix for Pork**

Drain peaches, reserving ¼ cup syrup. Moisten chops with reserved syrup. Add ginger to coating mix in shaker bag.

Shake 1 or 2 chops at a time with coating mix. Place in 15×10×1-inch baking pan. Discard any remaining mix.

Bake at 400°F for 15 minutes. Place peaches in pan. Bake an additional 5 minutes or until chops are cooked through. Garnish with thyme flowers.

Note: Bake thicker chops 5 to 10 minutes longer.

Lemon Dill Fish

Prep time: 5 minutes   Broiling time: 16 minutes

Makes 4 servings

½   cup KRAFT Mayo Real Mayonnaise
1   to 2 tablespoons lemon juice
1   teaspoon dill weed
½   teaspoon grated lemon peel
1   pound firm-textured fish fillets (such as
     cod, catfish *or* salmon)

Mix mayo, juice, dill and peel.

Place fish on greased rack of broiler pan 2 to 4 inches from heat. Brush with ½ of the mayo mixture.

Broil 5 to 8 minutes. Turn; brush with remaining mayo mixture. Continue broiling 5 to 8 minutes or until fish flakes easily with fork. Garnish with lemon peel and fresh dill.

Kids Can Help

The benefits of enlisting kids as your mess officers are twofold. Following a simple recipe or your directions, they can fix the main course when you're running late, and they'll learn the essentials of meal preparation at the same time. What's more, they'll gobble up the delicious results.

Zesty Chicken *Pot Pie*

Prep time: 20 minutes   Baking time: 25 minutes

Makes 8 servings

2 packages (8 ounces *each*) PHILADELPHIA Cream Cheese, cubed
½ cup chicken broth
3 cups chopped cooked chicken *or* turkey
2 packages (10 ounces *each*) frozen mixed vegetables, thawed
2 envelopes GOOD SEASONS Italian *or* Zesty Italian Salad Dressing Mix
1 package (15 ounces) refrigerated pie crusts (2 crusts)

Melt cream cheese with broth in saucepan on low heat. Stir in chicken, vegetables and salad dressing mix.

Spoon into 9-inch pie plate. Cover with 1 pie crust; seal and flute edge. Cut several slits to permit steam to escape. Cut remaining pie crust into decorative shapes. Place on pie. Place pie plate on cookie sheet.

Bake at 425°F for 20 to 25 minutes or until golden brown.

Lower Fat Pot Pie: Prepare as directed, substituting PHILADELPHIA Neufchâtel Cheese, ⅓ Less Fat than Cream Cheese, for regular cream cheese.

To make ahead, prepare pie as directed except for baking. Wrap securely; freeze. When ready to serve, unwrap. Place strips of foil around edges to prevent overbrowning. Bake frozen pie at 425°F for 1 hour and 10 minutes or until thoroughly heated and golden brown.

Simple Chili

Prep time: 15 minutes   Cooking time: 20 minutes

Makes about 5 cups

1   **pound ground beef**
1   **green pepper, chopped**
1   **envelope GOOD SEASONS Zesty Italian**
      or Italian Salad Dressing Mix
2   **teaspoons chili powder**
1   **can (15 ounces) kidney beans, drained**
1   **cup water**
1   **can (8 ounces) tomato sauce**
1   **can (4 ounces) chopped green chilies,**
      drained

Brown meat in large skillet on medium heat. Add green pepper, salad dressing mix and chili powder; cook and stir until green pepper is tender.

Stir in kidney beans, water and tomato sauce. Bring to boil. Reduce heat to low; cover and simmer 5 minutes, stirring occasionally.

Stir in chilies; return to boil. Serve warm with shredded cheddar cheese, chopped onion or sour cream, if desired.

Dinner Check-In

To tell at a glance who'll be home for dinner, outfit your refrigerator door with a wipe-off slate that shows a week's worth of calendar squares. Ask everyone to note when she or he will be gone, and where; then, wipe the slate clean when you're back at home base.

Salsa Mac 'n Cheese

Prep time: 10 minutes Cooking time: 15 minutes

Makes 4 to 6 servings

1	**pound ground beef**
1	**jar (16 ounces) TACO BELL HOME ORIGINALS Thick 'N Chunky Salsa**
1¾	**cups water**
2	**cups elbow macaroni, uncooked**
¾	**pound (12 ounces) VELVEETA Pasteurized Prepared Cheese Product, cut up**

Brown meat in large skillet; drain.

Stir in salsa and water. Bring to boil. Stir in macaroni. Reduce heat to medium-low; cover. Simmer 8 to 10 minutes or until macaroni is tender.

Add prepared cheese product; stir until melted.

Easy *Pasta Bake*

Prep time: 15 minutes   Baking time: 20 minutes

Makes 6 servings

1   **pound ground beef**
4   **cups mostaccioli, cooked, drained**
1   **jar (30 ounces) spaghetti sauce**
¾   **cup (3 ounces) KRAFT 100% Grated Parmesan Cheese, divided**
1   **package (8 ounces) KRAFT Shredded Low-Moisture Part-Skim Mozzarella Cheese**

Brown meat in large skillet; drain. Stir in mostaccioli, spaghetti sauce and ½ cup of Parmesan cheese.

Spoon into 13×9-inch baking dish. Top with mozzarella cheese and remaining ¼ cup Parmesan cheese.

Bake at 375°F for 20 minutes.

Lighter Pasta Bake: Omit meat, if desired. Prepare as directed, substituting KRAFT Shredded Reduced Fat Mozzarella Cheese for the mozzarella cheese and KRAFT FREE Nonfat Grated Topping for the Parmesan cheese.

Easy Turkey Primavera

Prep time: 5 minutes   Cooking time: 10 minutes

Makes 4 servings

1   pound LOUIS RICH Breast of Turkey, cut into strips
2   cups fresh broccoli flowerets
1   red pepper, cut in 1-inch chunks
6   fresh mushrooms, quartered
2   tablespoons water *or* white wine
1   package (10 ounces) DI GIORNO Four Cheese Alfredo Sauce *or* Alfredo Sauce
1   package (9 ounces) DI GIORNO Fettuccine, cooked, drained

Place turkey, broccoli, red pepper, mushrooms and water in skillet; cover.

Heat on medium heat 8 minutes or until vegetables are tender. Stir in sauce; heat 2 minutes.

Toss with hot cooked fettuccine.

Easy Turkey Primavera with Carrots: Prepare as directed, substituting 2 carrots, peeled, thinly sliced, for red pepper.

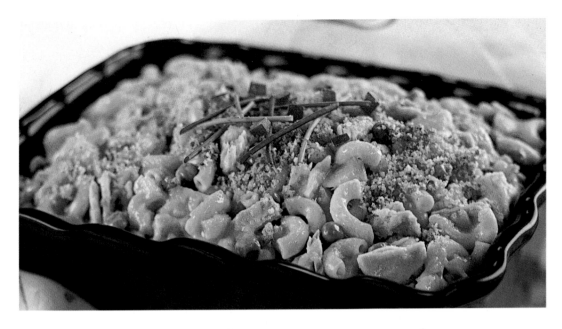

Homestyle *Tuna* Casserole

Prep time: 15 minutes   *Baking time: 35 minutes*

Makes 4 servings

1 **package (14 ounces) KRAFT Deluxe Macaroni & Cheese Dinner *or* KRAFT Light Deluxe Macaroni & Cheese Dinner**
1 **can (10¾ ounces) condensed cream of celery soup**
1 **cup frozen peas**
1 **can (6 ounces) tuna, drained, flaked**
½ **cup milk**
2 **tablespoons finely chopped onion**
2 **cups fresh bread crumbs**
¼ **cup (½ stick) butter *or* margarine, melted**

Prepare Dinner as directed on package. Add soup, peas, tuna, milk and onion; mix lightly.

Spoon into 2-quart casserole. Toss crumbs and butter; sprinkle over casserole.

Bake at 350°F for 30 to 35 minutes or until thoroughly heated. Garnish with fresh chives and chopped tomato.

To make ahead, prepare as directed except for baking; cover. Refrigerate overnight. When ready to serve, bake, uncovered, at 350°F for 1 hour or until thoroughly heated.

Cheesy Shells with Veggies

Prep time: 10 minutes   Cooking time: 12 minutes

Makes 4 servings

1 **package (12 ounces) VELVEETA Shells & Cheese Dinner**
1 **cup frozen mixed vegetables**
⅓ **cup chopped red pepper**
¼ **teaspoon dried thyme leaves**

Prepare Dinner as directed on package, adding vegetables during last 3 minutes of Macaroni cooking time.

Stir in remaining ingredients.

Cottage Cheese and *Vegetable* Topped Potato

Prep time: 10 minutes

Makes 1 serving

1   **hot baked potato, split**

½   **cup cooked sliced carrots, red pepper strips and halved sliced zucchini**

½   **cup BREAKSTONE'S *or* KNUDSEN Cottage Cheese**

Top potato with vegetables and cottage cheese. Garnish with fresh chives.

Ham 'n Potatoes *au Gratin*

Prep time: 30 minutes   Cooking time: 15 minutes

Makes 8 to 12 servings

½ cup *each* chopped green pepper and chopped onion
1   tablespoon butter *or* margarine
¾ pound (12 ounces) VELVEETA Pasteurized Prepared Cheese Product, cut up
⅓ cup milk
5   cups cubed cooked potatoes
1½ cups diced ham

Cook and stir green pepper and onion in butter in large skillet on medium-high heat until tender. Reduce heat to low. Add prepared cheese product and milk; stir until prepared cheese product is melted.

Stir in remaining ingredients; heat thoroughly, stirring occasionally.

Top a Pizza

Transform pizza crust into a hearty dinner by loading it up with delicious extras. For taco pizza, brown ground beef with TACO BELL HOME ORIGINALS Taco Seasoning Mix; add tomato sauce. Then, top with KRAFT Four Cheese Mexican Style Shredded Cheese, shredded lettuce, chopped tomato and TACO BELL HOME ORIGINALS Salsa. For barbecue pizza, spread with your favorite KRAFT Barbecue Sauce, shredded cooked chicken, sliced green onions and green pepper. Top with KRAFT Shredded Mozzarella Cheese.

Warm Chicken & Cranberry Salad

Prep time: 10 minutes   Cooking time: 10 minutes

Makes 4 servings

1   cup **KRAFT Special Collection Balsamic Vinaigrette Dressing, divided**
1   **pound boneless skinless chicken breasts, cut into strips**
1   **package (10 ounces) salad greens**
1   **cup dried cranberries *or* cherries**
¼   **cup sliced almonds, toasted**

Heat ¼ cup of the dressing in skillet on medium-high heat. Add chicken; cook and stir 8 minutes or until chicken is cooked through.

Toss chicken, greens, cranberries and almonds. Spoon onto serving platter. Drizzle with remaining ¾ cup dressing.

Sweet Orange & Chicken Salad

Prep time: 10 minutes   Broiling or grilling time: 10 minutes

Makes 6 servings

1   bottle (8 ounces) KRAFT CATALINA Dressing *or* KRAFT FREE CATALINA Fat Free Dressing, divided
4   boneless skinless chicken breast halves (about 1¼ pounds)
1   *each* red, yellow and green pepper, quartered
1   package (10 ounces) salad greens
2   oranges, peeled, sectioned
1   tablespoon toasted sesame seed

Brush ½ cup of the dressing on chicken and peppers.

Place on rack of broiler pan 2 to 3 inches from heat or on greased grill over hot coals. Broil or grill chicken and peppers 5 minutes on each side or until chicken is cooked through. Slice chicken diagonally into strips. Cut peppers into thin strips.

Toss chicken, peppers, greens, oranges and remaining dressing. Sprinkle with sesame seed.

Mix Your Own Greens

Combining greens makes a salad more interesting and often more nutritious. If you can't find a bag of mixed greens, just mix your own. Look for red and green leaf lettuce, arugula, raddichio, kale, spinach, romaine, butterhead or Boston lettuce.

Steak & Spinach Salad

Prep time: 10 minutes plus marinating   Grilling or broiling time: 20 minutes

Makes 4 servings

1 **envelope GOOD SEASONS Gourmet Parmesan Italian Salad Dressing Mix**
⅓ **cup apple cider vinegar**
⅓ **cup olive oil**
1 **clove garlic, minced**
1 **beef sirloin steak, ½ to ¾ inch thick (about 1 pound)**
8 **cups torn spinach**
1 **cup sliced mushrooms**
1 **large tomato, cut into wedges**
¼ **cup sliced green onions**

Mix salad dressing mix, vinegar, olive oil and garlic in cruet or small bowl as directed on envelope. Reserve ⅓ cup of the dressing mixture; refrigerate.

Pour remaining dressing over steak; cover. Refrigerate 1 hour to marinate. Drain; discard dressing mixture.

Place steak on greased grill over hot coals or on rack of broiler pan 2 to 3 inches from heat. Grill or broil 10 minutes on each side or to desired doneness. Cut into slices.

Toss spinach, mushrooms, tomato and onions with reserved ⅓ cup dressing mixture. Arrange steak slices over salad.

Chicken & Spinach Salad: Prepare as directed, substituting 1 pound boneless skinless chicken breasts for steak.

Crunchy Turkey Sandwich *Melts*

Prep time: 10 minutes   Baking time: 15 minutes

Makes 4 servings

2 **cups chopped cooked turkey**
½ **cup KRAFT Shredded Mild Cheddar Cheese**
⅓ **cup KRAFT Mayo Light Mayonnaise**
2 **tablespoons finely chopped onion**
2 **teaspoons KRAFT Pure Prepared Mustard**
¼ **teaspoon pepper**
8 **to 12 CLAUSSEN Sandwich Slices**
4 **sandwich *or* hamburger buns**

Mix turkey, cheese, mayo, onion, mustard and pepper.

Arrange 2 or 3 pickle slices on bottom half of each bun. Top each with ½ cup turkey mixture and top half of bun. Place sandwiches on ungreased cookie sheet; cover tightly with foil.

Bake at 350°F for 15 minutes.

Grilled Ham & Cheese

Prep time: 5 minutes   Cooking time: 10 minutes

Makes 1 sandwich

2   slices bread
2   KRAFT Singles Process Cheese Food
3   slices OSCAR MAYER Smoked Cooked
Ham
MIRACLE WHIP Salad Dressing *or* KRAFT
Mayo Real Mayonnaise

Top 1 bread slice with 1 process cheese food slice, ham, second process cheese food slice and second bread slice.

Spread outside of sandwich with salad dressing or mayo.

Cook in skillet on medium heat until lightly browned on both sides.

Dressed-Up Grilled Ham & Cheese: Prepare as directed, spreading bread with Dijon mustard and adding tomato slices before cooking.

Round Out the Meal

Turn a simple main dish into a complete meal with one of these handy ideas using KRAFT products.

• Serve your favorite KRAFT dressing with 1 package (10 ounces) mixed salad greens or pre-cut carrots and celery sticks.

• Pour heated CHEEZ WHIZ Pasteurized Process Cheese Sauce over steamed cut-up broccoli.

• Brush the cut sides of split French bread with cooking oil. Sprinkle with KRAFT 100% Grated Parmesan Cheese. Bake until lightly browned.

• For an easy ready-to-eat dessert, try JELL-O Gelatin Snacks or JELL-O Pudding Snacks. For an added treat, stir chopped nuts, granola, chopped candy bars or fruit into the pudding snacks.

Cheesy Vegetable Grills

Prep time: 5 minutes   Cooking time: 10 minutes

Makes 4 sandwiches

8   slices whole grain bread
4   teaspoons Dijon mustard
¼   pound (4 ounces) VELVEETA Pasteurized
**   Prepared Cheese Product, sliced**
1   green pepper, cut into rings
4   thin onion slices
4   slices tomato
8   teaspoons butter *or* margarine,
**   softened**

Spread 1 side of 4 bread slices each with 1 teaspoon mustard. Top with prepared cheese product, green pepper, onion, tomato and second bread slice.

Spread sandwiches with 1 teaspoon butter on each outer side. Cook in large skillet on medium heat until lightly browned on both sides.

Smoked Turkey *Broccoli* Calzones

Prep time: 10 minutes   Baking time: 15 minutes

Makes 4 servings

1   **package (10 ounces) frozen chopped broccoli, thawed, drained**
1   **package (6 ounces) LOUIS RICH Smoked Turkey Breast, chopped**
1   **cup KRAFT Shredded Cheddar Cheese**
1   **plum tomato, seeded, chopped**
½   **cup KRAFT Mayo: Real *or* Light Mayonnaise**
2   **cans (10 ounces *each*) pizza crust dough**

Mix all ingredients except dough.

Roll out dough. Cut each crust in half diagonally. Spoon ¾ cup of the filling on each crust half. Fold over; crimp edges closed with fork. Place on greased cookie sheet.

Bake at 425°F for 12 to 15 minutes or until golden brown.

Chicken *Enchiladas*

Prep time: 20 minutes   Baking time: 35 minutes

Makes 6 servings

2 **cups chopped cooked chicken *or* turkey**
1 **container (16 ounces) BREAKSTONE'S *or* KNUDSEN Sour Cream, divided**
1 **package (8 ounces) KRAFT Shredded Colby & Monterey Jack Cheese, divided**
1 **jar (16 ounces) TACO BELL HOME ORIGINALS Thick 'N Chunky Salsa, divided**
2 **tablespoons chopped cilantro *or* dried parsley**
12 **flour *or* corn tortillas (6 to 8 inch)**

Mix chicken, 1 cup of the sour cream, 1 cup of the cheese, ¼ cup of the salsa and cilantro.

Spoon about ¼ cup of the chicken mixture down center of each tortilla; roll up. Place, seam-side down, in 13×9-inch baking dish. Top with remaining salsa; cover.

Bake at 350°F for 30 minutes. Sprinkle with remaining cheese. Bake an additional 5 minutes or until cheese is melted. Serve with remaining sour cream. Garnish with additional chopped cilantro.

Cheesy Chicken Fajitas

Prep time: 15 minutes   Cooking time: 10 minutes

Makes 6 servings

½ **pound boneless skinless chicken breasts, cut into thin strips**
1 **clove garlic, minced**
1 **medium green *and/or* red pepper, cut into strips**
½ **cup sliced onion**
1½ **cups KRAFT Four Cheese Mexican Style Shredded Cheese**
6 **flour tortillas (6 inch), warmed**
  TACO BELL HOME ORIGINALS Thick 'N Chunky Salsa

Spray skillet with no stick cooking spray. Add chicken and garlic; cook on medium-high heat 5 minutes.

Add green pepper and onion; cook 4 to 5 minutes or until tender-crisp.

Place ¼ cup chicken mixture and ¼ cup cheese on center of each tortilla; fold. Serve with salsa and lime wedges.

VELVEETA®
Vegetable Bake
(recipe, page 206)

Favorite Spinach
Salad (recipe, page
219)

Brown Rice
Amandine (recipe,
page 207)

MIX-AND-MATCH
SIDE DISHES

No-fuss accompaniments are the

perfect way to dress up your holiday

meals. This enticing assortment of salads,

vegetable medleys, stuffings and rice and

pasta dishes includes everything from

new-fashioned Pear & Pecan Salad with

Mixed Greens to two simple fix-ups for

all-time favorite mashed potatoes.

VELVEETA® *Vegetable* Bake

(Photo on pages 204–205.)

Prep time: 5 minutes   Baking time: 30 minutes

Makes 4 to 6 servings

1 **package (16 ounces) frozen broccoli cuts, partially cooked, drained**
¾ **pound (12 ounces) VELVEETA Pasteurized Prepared Cheese Product, cut up**
¾ **cup crushed buttery crackers**
2 **tablespoons butter *or* margarine**

Mix broccoli and prepared cheese product. Spoon into greased 1½-quart casserole. Sprinkle with crushed crackers; dot with butter.

Bake at 375°F for 25 to 30 minutes or until thoroughly heated.

Bread with a Zing

For a flavorful and crispy bread fix-up to accompany a variety of main dishes, prepare your favorite GOOD SEASONS Salad Dressing Mix and brush some dressing on French bread slices. Then, toast the slices as you would garlic bread.

Brown Rice Amandine

(Photo on pages 204–205.)

Prep time: 10 minutes   Microwave time: 10 minutes plus standing

Makes 6 servings

1½ cups MINUTE Instant Brown Rice, uncooked
1¼ cups chicken broth
1 medium onion, chopped
1 tablespoon lemon juice
1 tablespoon butter *or* margarine
2 teaspoons chopped fresh dill *or* ½ teaspoon dill weed
1 clove garlic, minced
1 cup frozen cut green beans, thawed
2 tablespoons toasted sliced almonds

Mix rice, broth, onion, juice, butter, dill and garlic in 2-quart microwavable casserole; cover.

Microwave on HIGH 5 minutes. Stir in beans; cover.

Microwave 5 minutes. Let stand 5 minutes. Stir in almonds. Garnish with lemon slices and additional fresh dill.

Sausage Stuffing

Prep time: 10 minutes   Cooking time: 10 minutes plus standing

Makes about 5 cups stuffing or 10 servings

¼ pound bulk pork sausage
1 cup sliced celery
1 cup sliced mushrooms (about ¼ pound)
1 small onion, chopped
1½ cups beef broth
1 teaspoon poultry seasoning
½ teaspoon salt
1½ cups MINUTE White *or* Premium Long Grain Rice, uncooked

Brown sausage in saucepan or skillet on medium-high heat. Add celery, mushrooms and onion; cook and stir 3 minutes.

Stir in broth, seasoning and salt. Bring to boil. Stir in rice; cover. Remove from heat. Let stand 5 minutes.

Pasta Bow Ties with *Spinach* and Bacon

Prep time: 15 minutes   Cooking time: 15 minutes

Makes 12 servings

1 **package (12 ounces) bow tie pasta, uncooked**
2 **tablespoons olive oil**
2 **cloves garlic, chopped**
1 **package (10 ounces) frozen chopped spinach, thawed**
½ **cup dry white wine**
⅓ **cup KRAFT 100% Grated Parmesan Cheese**
1 **package (12 ounces) OSCAR MAYER Center Cut Bacon, crisply cooked, crumbled**
Pepper (optional)

Cook pasta as directed on package. Drain pasta, reserving ½ cup cooking water.

Heat oil and garlic in large skillet on medium heat 1 minute. Increase heat to medium-high; add spinach, wine and reserved ½ cup cooking water. Cook and stir until thoroughly heated.

Toss pasta and cheese with spinach mixture; sprinkle with bacon. Season to taste with pepper.

Fettuccine Alfeta

Prep time: 10 minutes   Cooking time: 10 minutes

Makes 6 servings

12 **ounces fettuccine, uncooked**
3 **tablespoons olive oil**
1 **package (8 ounces) ATHENOS Feta Cheese with Basil & Tomato, crumbled**
2 **cups chopped tomatoes**
¼ **cup julienne-cut fresh basil *or* 2 teaspoons dried basil leaves**

Cook fettuccine as directed on package for 8 to 10 minutes or until al dente. (Pasta should be tender when bitten, but still firm.) Drain. Return to pan; toss with oil.

Toss with cheese, tomatoes and basil. Season to taste with salt and pepper.

**Pasta Bow Ties with
Spinach and Bacon
(recipe opposite page)**

Twice Baked Potatoes

Prep time: 10 minutes   Baking time: 20 minutes

Makes 4 servings

4   **medium potatoes, baked**
1   **cup BREAKSTONE'S *or* KNUDSEN Sour Cream**
1   **cup KRAFT Shredded Cheddar Cheese**
¼   **cup *each* milk and sliced green onions**
1   **envelope GOOD SEASONS Gourmet Parmesan Italian *or* Cheese Garlic Salad Dressing Mix**

Cut potatoes in half lengthwise; scoop out centers leaving ¼-inch shells.

Mash potatoes. Stir in sour cream, cheese, milk, onions and salad dressing mix. Spoon into shells. Place on cookie sheet.

Bake at 325°F for 15 to 20 minutes.

Green Onions or Scallions?

No matter if you call them green onions or scallions, these fresh onions with a white end and long green shoots add a deliciously mild onion flavor to foods. To use them, trim off the roots and remove any wilted, brown or damaged tops; then slice and use as much of the white end and green shoot as you like.

Quick Cheesy *Mashed Potatoes*

Prep time: 20 minutes

Makes 6 servings

4 **cups hot cooked sliced potatoes**
½ **pound (8 ounces) VELVEETA Pasteurized Prepared Cheese Product, cut up**

Mash potatoes coarsely with fork or potato masher.

Add prepared cheese product. Mash until prepared cheese product is melted and potatoes are desired consistency.

Season to taste with salt and pepper. Garnish as desired. Serve immediately.

Jazzy Mashed Potatoes

(Photo on pages 218.)

Prep time: 20 minutes

Makes 8 servings

4 **cups hot prepared mashed potatoes**
1 **cup BREAKSTONE'S *or* KNUDSEN Sour Cream**
2 **tablespoons OSCAR MAYER Real Bacon Bits**

Mix all ingredients. Garnish with chive flowers. Serve immediately.

Gourmet Grilled Vegetable Salad

Prep time: 10 minutes   Grilling time: 30 minutes or Stovetop cooking time: 15 minutes

Makes 6 servings

¼   **cup apple cider vinegar**
2   **tablespoons water**
1   **envelope GOOD SEASONS Gourmet Parmesan Italian *or* Italian Salad Dressing Mix**
⅓   **cup olive oil**
1   **pound small red potatoes, cut into quarters**
1   ***each* zucchini and yellow squash, halved lengthwise, cut into ½-inch chunks**
1   **cup slivered red onion**

Mix vinegar, water, salad dressing mix and oil in cruet or small bowl as directed on envelope. Toss with vegetables.

Spoon mixture evenly onto double layer of heavy-duty aluminum foil; close foil to form tightly sealed pouch.

Place pouch on greased grill over medium coals. Grill 30 minutes, turning and shaking pouch halfway through grilling time. Garnish with fresh rosemary.

To cook on stove: Prepare dressing as directed; set aside. Boil potatoes in 6 quarts water for 10 minutes. Add zucchini, squash and onion; boil 5 minutes or until vegetables are tender. Drain; toss with dressing. Serve immediately.

Praline *Sweet* Potatoes

Prep time: 45 minutes   Baking time: 30 minutes

Makes 8 servings

2	**pounds sweet potatoes, cooked, peeled and mashed**
½	**cup MIRACLE WHIP Salad Dressing**
½	**cup firmly packed brown sugar, divided**
1	**teaspoon ground ginger**
¼	**teaspoon grated orange peel**
¼	**cup chopped pecans**
1	**tablespoon butter *or* margarine, softened**
¼	**teaspoon ground cinnamon**

Mix sweet potatoes, salad dressing, ¼ cup of the sugar, ginger and peel. Spoon into 1½-quart casserole.

Mix remaining ¼ cup sugar, pecans, butter and cinnamon; sprinkle over potato mixture.

Bake at 350°F for 30 minutes. Garnish with orange peel and fresh herb.

Cranberry Cream Cheese Mold

Prep time: 30 minutes   Refrigerating time: 6 hours

Makes 12 servings

1½   **cups boiling water**
1   **package (8-serving size) *or* 2 packages (4-serving size *each*) JELL-O Cranberry Flavor Gelatin *or* Cranberry Flavor Sugar Free Low Calorie Gelatin Dessert *or* any red flavor**
1½   **cups cold water**
½   **teaspoon ground cinnamon**
1   **medium apple, chopped**
1   **cup whole berry cranberry sauce (optional)**
1   **package (8 ounces) PHILADELPHIA Cream Cheese *or* PHILADELPHIA Neufchâtel Cheese, ⅓ Less Fat than Cream Cheese, softened**

Stir boiling water into gelatin in large bowl 2 minutes or until completely dissolved. Stir in cold water and cinnamon.

Pour 2 cups of the gelatin into medium bowl. Refrigerate about 1½ hours or until thickened. (Spoon drawn through leaves a definite impression.) Reserve remaining 1 cup gelatin at room temperature.

Stir apple and cranberry sauce into thickened gelatin. Spoon into 6-cup mold. Refrigerate about 30 minutes or until set but not firm. (Gelatin should stick to your finger when touched and should mound.)

Stir reserved 1 cup gelatin gradually into cream cheese in small bowl with wire whisk until smooth. Pour over gelatin layer in mold.

Refrigerate 4 hours or until firm. Unmold (tip, page 216). Garnish as desired. Store leftover gelatin mold in refrigerator.

Sparkling Fruit Mold

Prep time: 15 minutes   Refrigerating time: 4¾ hours

Makes 12 servings

1½ **cups boiling water**
 1 **package (6 ounces) *or* 2 packages
      (3 ounces *each*) JELL-O Sparkling
      White Grape Flavor Gelatin Dessert**
 2 **cups cold ginger ale**
½ **cup *each* red and green grape halves**
 1 **can (11 ounces) mandarin orange
      segments, drained**

Stir boiling water into gelatin in large bowl at least 2 minutes until completely dissolved. Refrigerate 15 minutes. Gently stir in cold ginger ale. Refrigerate about 30 minutes or until slightly thickened. (Gelatin is consistency of unbeaten egg whites.) Gently stir for 15 seconds. Stir in grapes and oranges. Pour into 6-cup mold.

Refrigerate 4 hours or until firm. Unmold. Garnish as desired.

Unmolding Gelatin

After refrigerating a gelatin mold until completely firm, follow these steps for unmolding the mold with ease.

• Moisten fingertip and gently pull gelatin from top edge of mold.

• Dip mold in warm, not hot, water, just to rim, for about 15 seconds.

• Lift mold from water, hold upright and shake to loosen gelatin.

• Moisten chilled serving plate with water. (This allows gelatin to be moved after unmolding.) Place moistened serving plate upside down on top of mold.

• Invert mold and plate; holding mold and plate together, shake slightly to loosen.

• Gently remove mold. If gelatin does not release easily, dip mold in warm water again for a few seconds. Remove mold; center gelatin on serving plate.

Jazzy Mashed
Potatoes (recipe,
page 211)

Pear & Pecan Salad
with Mixed Greens
(recipe opposite page)

Favorite Spinach Salad

(Photo on pages 204–205.)

Prep time: 15 minutes

Makes 6 servings

5 cups torn spinach
2 cups sliced mushrooms
1 can (8 ounces) sliced water chestnuts, drained
1 cup bean sprouts
½ cup thinly sliced red onion wedges
4 slices OSCAR MAYER Bacon, crisply cooked, crumbled
2 hard-cooked eggs, chopped
¾ cup KRAFT CATALINA Dressing

Toss all ingredients except dressing in large bowl.

Serve with dressing.

Pear & Pecan Salad with *Mixed Greens*

Prep time: 15 minutes

Makes about 10 servings

1 package (10 ounces) salad greens
2 medium pears, cored and sliced
1 cup seedless red grapes
1 bottle (8 ounces) KRAFT Ranch Dressing *or* KRAFT FREE Ranch Fat Free Dressing
⅓ cup pecan *or* walnut halves, toasted
KRAFT Blue Cheese Crumbles (optional)

Toss greens, pears and grapes in large bowl.

Drizzle with dressing and top with pecans and cheese just before serving.

Bacon Ranch Bread Bites

Prep time: 10 minutes plus rising   Baking time: 30 minutes

Makes 10 servings

1   **loaf frozen bread dough, thawed**
2   **teaspoons olive oil**
1   **package (12 ounces) OSCAR MAYER Center Cut Bacon, cut into 1-inch pieces, cooked not crisp, drained**
1   **cup KRAFT Shredded Low-Moisture Part-Skim Mozzarella Cheese**
1   **envelope ranch salad dressing mix**

Roll bread dough into ½-inch-thick rectangle. Brush top of dough with oil. Cut dough with sharp knife into 1-inch pieces.

Toss bread dough pieces, bacon, cheese and salad dressing mix in large bowl. Place on ungreased cookie sheet; shape into low oval loaf. Let rise until double in size.

Bake at 350°F for 20 to 30 minutes or until golden brown.

PARM PLUS!® *Breadsticks*

Prep time: 10 minutes   Baking time: 18 minutes

Makes 16

1   **can (11 ounces) refrigerated soft breadsticks**

3   **tablespoons butter *or* margarine, melted**

½   **cup PARM PLUS! Seasoning Blend**

Separate and cut breadstick dough into 16 breadsticks.

Dip in butter; coat with seasoning blend. Twist; place on ungreased cookie sheet.

Bake at 350°F for 14 to 18 minutes or until golden brown.

Pumpkin Cupcakes
(recipe, page 227)

HALLOWEEN FAMILY FUN

Whether it's a big get-together set at a pumpkin patch or a small family gathering in your living room, a Halloween party is guaranteed to be fun for all. It's easy to get in the bewitching spirit with this bonus section of *tricks*, such as Ghostly Jokes, *and treats,* including Goblin Goo Drink and Witch's Web dessert.

Ghosts in the Graveyard

Prep time: 10 minutes plus refrigerating
Makes 15 to 18 servings

1 **package (16 ounces) chocolate sandwich cookies**
3½ **cups cold milk**
2 **packages (4-serving size each) JELL-O Chocolate Flavor Instant Pudding & Pie Filling**
1 **tub (12 ounces) COOL WHIP Whipped Topping, thawed**

Crush cookies in zipper-style plastic bag with rolling pin or in food processor.

Pour cold milk into large bowl. Add pudding mixes. Beat with wire whisk 2 minutes. Gently stir in 3 cups of the whipped topping and ½ of the crushed cookies. Spoon into 13×9-inch dish. Sprinkle with remaining crushed cookies.

Refrigerate 1 hour or until ready to serve. Store leftover dessert, covered, in refrigerator.

To Decorate Graveyard:
Decorate assorted cookies with decorating icings or gels to create "tombstones." Stand "tombstones" on top of dessert with candy corn, candy pumpkins and tiny jelly beans. Drop remaining whipped topping by spoonfuls onto dessert to create ghosts. Decorate with candies to create "eyes."

Boo Cups:

Layer pudding mixture, remaining crushed cookies and candy corn or tiny jelly beans in 12 to 16 glasses or clear plastic cups. Decorate with additional candies, decorated cookies and whipped topping, as desired. Makes 12 to 16 servings.

Spooky *Eyeball* Tacos

Prep time: 15 minutes   *Baking time: 20 minutes*
Makes 12 servings

1 **pound ground beef**
1 **package (10 ¾ ounces)**
   TACO BELL HOME ORIGINALS
   Taco Dinner Kit
   Shredded lettuce
   Chopped tomatoes
   BREAKSTONE'S *or* KNUDSEN
   Sour Cream

Mix meat and Seasoning Mix. Shape into 36 (1-inch) balls; place in 13×9-inch baking dish. Bake at 350°F for 15 to 20 minutes or until cooked through.

Fill each of 12 Taco Shells with 1 meatball, Taco Sauce, lettuce and tomato.

Top with 2 additional meatballs dipped in sour cream. Garnish with sliced pitted ripe olives to create "eyes." Makes 12 servings.

Note: You can make the meatballs ahead and freeze in a zipper-style plastic freezer bag. To reheat, open bag slightly; microwave on HIGH 2 minutes.

Devilishly Delicious Snacks

Keep hungry Halloween revelers happy with this quick-to-put-together snack. Spread PHILADELPHIA FLAVORS Cheesecake Flavor Cream Cheese Spread on cinnamon or plain graham crackers or vanilla wafer cookies. Decorate with Halloween sprinkles, if desired.

Witch's Web

Prep time: 15 minutes plus refrigerating

Makes 15 servings

2 **packages (12.6 ounces *each*)
JELL-O No Bake Cookies &
Creme Dessert**
⅔ **cup butter *or* margarine,
melted**
2⅔ **cups cold milk**

Stir Crust Mix and butter
thoroughly with spoon in
13×9-inch pan until crumbs are
well moistened. Press firmly onto
bottom of pan.

Pour cold milk into deep, narrow-
bottom bowl. Add Filling Mix. Beat
with electric mixer on low speed
30 seconds. Beat on high speed
3 minutes. DO NOT UNDERBEAT.
Stir Crushed Cookies into filling
until well blended. Spread filling
mixture over crust. Garnish with
decorating icing and candies to
create "spiderweb" and "spider."

Refrigerate at least 1 hour or
until set. To serve, dip bottom of
pan in hot water for 30 seconds for
easier cutting and serving. Cover;
store leftover dessert in refrigerator.

Creative Carving

Here are a few general hints for pumpkin carving:

- Draw a face on the pumpkin with markers before you start to carve.
- Cut the top of the pumpkin off at an angle so the top won't fall through when the heat of the candle starts to shrivel up the pumpkin. Or, don't even cut the top off! Just cut out a hole in the back, scoop out the seeds and slide the candle through the hole.

- To keep the candle standing up straight, secure it in melted wax on a jar lid.

- If you like, carve several jack-o'-lanterns and group them together—it will be more dramatic than just one pumpkin.

Pumpkin *Cupcakes*

(Photo on pages 222–223.)

Prep time: 15 minutes   Baking time: 20 minutes plus cooling

Makes 24 cupcakes

1   package (2-layer size) white cake mix *or* cake mix with pudding in the mix
¼   cup KOOL-AID Orange Flavor Sugar-Sweetened Soft Drink Mix
1   container (16 ounces) ready-to-spread vanilla frosting*

Prepare and bake cake mix as directed on package for cupcakes, adding soft drink mix before beating.

Frost cooled cupcakes with frosting. Sprinkle with additional soft drink mix to resemble pumpkins. Create a "face" with Halloween candies, decorating gel and decorating icing.

***Note:** To color frosting, stir 1 tablespoon KOOL-AID Orange Flavor Sugar-Sweetened Soft Drink Mix into frosting until well blended.

Goblin Goo
Drink (recipe
opposite page)

Two Color Goo
(recipe opposite page)

Goblin Goo Drink

Prep time: 15 minutes   Refrigerating time: 4 hours

Makes 8 servings

1   **package (8-serving size) or
    2 packages (4-serving size
    each) JELL-O Grape *or* Orange
    Flavor Gelatin Dessert**
4   **cups (1 quart) cold prepared
    KOOL-AID Grape *or* Orange
    Flavor Soft Drink Mix**

Prepare gelatin as directed
on package.

Refrigerate 4 hours or until
firm.

Break gelatin into small flakes
with fork. Spoon about ½ cup
gelatin into each of 8 tall glasses.

Pour ½ cup cold soft drink
over gelatin in each glass.
Serve immediately with a
straw to sip gelatin
pieces and soft drink.

Two Color Goo:

Prepare grape and orange
flavor gelatin as directed on
package. Refrigerate and break into
flakes as directed. Layer ¼ cup
orange (or grape) gelatin flakes,
¼ cup grape (or orange) gelatin
flakes and additional ¼ cup orange
(or grape) gelatin flakes in each
glass. Pour cold orange soft drink
over gelatin in each glass.

Fizzy Goblin Goo: Just before
serving, prepare KOOL-AID as
directed, substituting cold seltzer
for water.

Ghostly Jokes

All good little ghosts and
goblins need a supply of jokes
and riddles to share. Have you
heard these?
   Q. What did the ghost
receive when he won first
place at the fair? **A.** A boo
ribbon.
   Q. How do baby ghosts
keep their feet warm? **A.** They
wear BOOtees.
   Q. Knock, knock. **A.** Who's
there? **Q.** Boo! **A.** Boo who?
Q. Don't cry!
   Q. How do ghosts get to the
second floor? **A.** They take the
scares.

Candy Corn *Popcorn Balls*

Prep time: 15 minutes   Microwave time: 2 minutes

Makes 15

¼ **cup (½ stick) butter *or* margarine**
1 **package (10½ ounces) miniature marshmallows (6 cups)**
1 **package (4-serving size) JELL-O Gelatin Dessert, any flavor**
12 **cups (3 quarts) popped popcorn**
1 **cup candy corn**

Microwave butter and marshmallows in large microwavable bowl on HIGH 1½ to 2 minutes or until marshmallows are puffed. Stir in gelatin until well mixed.

Pour marshmallow mixture over popcorn and candy corn in large bowl. Mix lightly until well coated. Shape into 15 balls or other shapes with greased or wet hands. Wrap each ball in plastic wrap and tie with raffia or ribbon, if desired.

BOOlogna Snackers

White bread slices (optional)
OSCAR MAYER Bologna Slices
KRAFT Singles Process Cheese
Food

Alternate layers of bread, bologna and process cheese food on cutting board.

Cut into decorative shapes using Halloween-shaped cookie cutters or sharp knife.

Decorate with KRAFT Pure Prepared Mustard, catsup and cut-up process cheese food.

231

TACO BELL® HOME ORIGINALS™ 2-Step Taco Dip

Makes 6 to 8 servings

You only need:

1 container (16 ounces) BREAKSTONE'S *or* KNUDSEN Sour Cream

1 package (1¼ ounces) TACO BELL HOME ORIGINALS Taco Seasoning Mix

1 cup *each* shredded lettuce and chopped tomato

1 cup KRAFT Four Cheese Mexican Style Shredded Cheese

1. Prep It Quick! Mix sour cream and seasoning mix until well blended. Spread on bottom of 9-inch pie plate or quiche dish.

2. Pile On the Fun!™ Layer remaining ingredients over sour cream mixture. Garnish with green pepper cut-outs, sliced pitted ripe olives, small halved tomato slice and fresh chives to create a "cat's face." Serve with tortilla chips.

Fresh Air Halloween

Break with tradition and celebrate this Halloween outdoors. Create a buffet by arranging bales of straw into a table or using a picnic table. Then set out lots of nibble or finger foods so your hungry guests can stop by between activities to sample the treats.

METRIC COOKING HINTS

By making a few conversions, cooks in Australia, Canada and the United Kingdom can use these recipes with confidence. The charts on this page provide a guide for converting measurements from the U.S. customary system, which is used throughout this book, to the imperial and metric systems. There also is a conversion table for oven temperatures to accommodate the differences in oven calibrations.

Product Differences: Most of the ingredients called for in the recipes in this book are available in English-speaking countries. However, some are known by different names. Here are some common American ingredients and their possible counterparts:
■ Sugar is granulated or castor sugar.
■ Powdered sugar is icing sugar.
■ All-purpose flour is plain household flour or white flour. When self-rising flour is used in place of all-purpose flour in a recipe that calls for leavening, omit the leavening agent (baking soda or baking powder) and salt.
■ Light-colored corn syrup is golden syrup.
■ Cornstarch is cornflour.
■ Baking soda is bicarbonate of soda.
■ Vanilla is vanilla essence.
■ Green, red or yellow peppers are capsicums.
■ Golden raisins are sultanas.

Volume and Weight: Americans traditionally use cup measures for liquid and solid ingredients. The chart, below, shows the approximate imperial and metric equivalents. If you are accustomed to weighing solid ingredients, the following approximate equivalents will be helpful.
■ 1 cup butter, castor sugar or rice = 8 ounces = about 250 grams
■ 1 cup flour = 4 ounces = about 125 grams
■ 1 cup icing sugar = 5 ounces = about 150 grams
  Spoon measures are used for smaller amounts of ingredients. Although the size of the tablespoon varies slightly in different countries, for practical purposes and for recipes in this book, a straight substitution is all that's necessary.
  Measurements made using cups or spoons always should be level unless stated otherwise.

EQUIVALENTS: U.S. = AUSTRALIA/U.K.

$\frac{1}{8}$ teaspoon = 0.5 ml
$\frac{1}{4}$ teaspoon = 1 ml
$\frac{1}{2}$ teaspoon = 2 ml
1 teaspoon = 5 ml
1 tablespoon = 1 tablespoon
$\frac{1}{4}$ cup = 2 tablespoons = 2 fluid ounces = 60 ml
$\frac{1}{3}$ cup = $\frac{1}{4}$ cup = 3 fluid ounces = 90 ml
$\frac{1}{2}$ cup = $\frac{1}{3}$ cup = 4 fluid ounces = 120 ml
$\frac{2}{3}$ cup = $\frac{1}{2}$ cup = 5 fluid ounces = 150 ml
$\frac{3}{4}$ cup = $\frac{2}{3}$ cup = 6 fluid ounces = 180 ml
1 cup = $\frac{3}{4}$ cup = 8 fluid ounces = 240 ml
$1\frac{1}{4}$ cups = 1 cup
2 cups = 1 pint
1 quart = 1 liter
$\frac{1}{2}$ inch = 1.27 cm
1 inch = 2.54 cm

BAKING PAN SIZES

American	Metric
8×1½-inch round baking pan	20×4-cm cake tin
9×1½-inch round baking pan	23×3.5-cm cake tin
11×7×1½-inch baking pan	28×18×4-cm baking tin
13×9×2-inch baking pan	30×20×3-cm baking tin
2-quart rectangular baking dish	30×20×3-cm baking tin
15×10×1-inch baking pan	30×25×2-cm baking tin (Swiss roll tin)
9-inch pie plate	22×4- or 23×4-cm pie plate
7- or 8-inch springform pan	18- or 20-cm springform or loose-bottom cake tin
9×5×3-inch loaf pan	23×13×7-cm or 2-pound narrow loaf tin or pâté tin
1½-quart casserole	1.5-liter casserole
2-quart casserole	2-liter casserole

OVEN TEMPERATURE EQUIVALENTS

Fahrenheit Setting	Celsius Setting*	Gas Setting
300°F	150°C	Gas Mark 2 (slow)
325°F	160°C	Gas Mark 3 (moderately slow)
350°F	180°C	Gas Mark 4 (moderate)
375°F	190°C	Gas Mark 5 (moderately hot)
400°F	200°C	Gas Mark 6 (hot)
425°F	220°C	Gas Mark 7
450°F	230°C	Gas Mark 8 (very hot)
Broil		Grill

*Electric and gas ovens may be calibrated using Celsius. However, for an electric oven, increase the Celsius setting 10 to 20 degrees when cooking above 160°C. For convection or forced-air ovens (gas or electric), lower the temperature setting 10°C when cooking at all heat levels.